PRIVACY FOR BUSINESS:™
WEB SITES AND EMAIL

Privacy for Business™: Web Sites and Email

ISBN 0-9724819-0-7

Published in the U.S.A. by:
Dreva Hill, LLC
P.O. Box 3792
Saint Augustine, FL 32085
www.drevahill.com

Printed in the U.S.A. by:
Signature Book Printing
Gaithersburg, Maryland
www.sbpbooks.com

Cover Design by Dreva Hill and Blue Ruby.

For press review copies, sales inquiries, volume purchases, and corporate editions of this book, please contact drevahill@yahoo.com.

Library of Congress Control Number: 2002094963.

PRIVACY FOR BUSINESS
WEB SITES AND EMAIL

Stephen Cobb

Dreva Hill

For Brothers

C.A.C

1923-1973

D.T.C.

1921-1999

CONTENTS-AT-A-GLANCE

INTRODUCTION .... *XIV*

1: PRIVACY AND BUSINESS TODAY *3*

2: PRIVACY INCIDENTS AND THEIR COSTS *27*

3: WEB PRIVACY PRINCIPLES *55*

4: PRIVACY LAWS *75*

5: PRIVACY LAWS WORLDWIDE *96*

6: POLICIES, NOTICES AND STATEMENTS *109*

7: STRATEGY AND INCIDENT RESPONSE *129*

8: PRIVACY AND EMAIL *157*

9: TOOLS, SEALS, TECHNIQUES *189*

10: SUMMING UP *211*

SOURCES *219*

THE VALUE OF PRIVACY FOR BUSINESS

"The Royal Bank of Canada takes the position that giving customers the level of privacy they want is a competitive differentiator...Each year, the bank surveys customers about the importance of branch services, customer service, and more than a dozen other items. It added privacy to the list six years ago, and it ranks in the middle of what consumers consider valuable. Based on survey results, the bank figures that privacy drives 7% of the demand for its products and services. That means 7% of the $9.0billion shareholder value of the bank's consumer business: $630 million."

—"Royal Bank Of Canada Puts A Value On Privacy," Rick Whiting, *Information Week*, August 19, 2002.

TABLE OF CONTENTS

1: PRIVACY AND BUSINESS TODAY 3

Privacy Today 3
Privacy Questions 5
What is Web Privacy? 8
    Data Ownership 9
    Privacy Acronyms 11
    Legal Angles 14
Privacy Positives 16
Privacy Paradoxes 17
The Privacy Landscape 20
Privacy Policies and Statements 22
What's Next? 24

2: PRIVACY INCIDENTS AND THEIR COSTS 27

Defining "Privacy Incident" 27
The Costs of a Privacy Incident 28
    Scrutiny and Glare 28
    Settlement Costs 30
    Coping Costs 32
    Opportunity Costs 33
    Cost Limits and Gaps 34
    Fines and Other Costs 37
Types of Privacy Incident 39
    Security Breach 39
    Policy Violation 43

Policy Change 45
Policy Criticism 47
Consumer Costs 49
Aggravation 49
Identity Theft 49
Loss of Privacy 51

3: WEB PRIVACY PRINCIPLES 55

Basic Privacy Principles 55
Early U.S. Laws 56
The Hew Report 57
The OECD Guidelines 59
Data Controller 61
Transborder Data Flows 62
Fair Information Practice Principles 64
Notice/Awareness 65
Choice/Consent 67
Access/Participation 67
Integrity/Security 68
Enforcement/Redress 69
Options for Opting 69

4: PRIVACY LAWS 75

Children's Online Privacy Protection Act 75
What COPPA Requires 78
COPPA Implications 79
COPPA Safe Harbor 81
Gramm-Leach-Bliley 82
G-L-B Definitions 82
G-L-B and Pretexting 84
G-L-B Implications 84

G-L-B Response 86
Health Insurance Portability and Accountability Act 86
    What is HIPAA? 87
    Web Site Implications 89
    Broader Implications 91
Other Laws 93

5: PRIVACY LAWS WORLDWIDE 97

Global Considerations 97
Data Protection in the E.U. 98
The E.U. Data Protection Directive 99
U.S./E.U. Safe Harbor 101
    1. Notice 102
    2. Choice 102
    3. Onward Transfer 103
    4. Security 103
    5. Data Integrity 103
    6. Access 103
    7. Enforcement 104
The Value of Safe Harbor 105
    Other Safe Harbors 105

6: POLICIES, NOTICES AND STATEMENTS 109

Privacy Disclosures 109
Statement, Notice or Policy? 110
Practical Steps 111
    The Better Business Bureau Online 111
    TRUSTe 111
    The Direct Marketing Association 113
    The OECD 113

IAPO 113
Practical Issues *114*
    Mapping Data Flows 114
    Web Specific Issues 118
From Data to Policy and Back *119*
    High-Level Policy 121
    Internal v. External 122
From Policies Down to Procedures *123*
    From General to Online 124
    From External to Internal 124
    From Content Management to Privacy 125
Privacy Strategy *126*

7: STRATEGY AND INCIDENT RESPONSE 129

A Typical Privacy Scenario *129*
    Reality Check 130
    The Incident Meeting 131
    Privacy Investigator 132
    Problem Solving 134
    Lessons Learned 137
Enter the CPO *139*
    CPO Roles and Reporting 140
    Twin Roles 142
    Action Plan: Knowing, Saying, Doing 144
    Tips and Turf Wars 145
    The Privacy Team 147
Privacy Incident Response *148*
    The Privacy Incident Response Team 148
    The Privacy Incident Response Plan 150
    Seven Incident Response Steps 151
    Privacy Preparedness 152

8: PRIVACY AND EMAIL 157

The Tangled Email Web 157
The Spam Factor 158
The Economics of Spam 159
Spam Filters and Block Lists 161
The Size of Spam 165

Email and Privacy 167
Email Headers 169
Spam and Privacy 172
The Anti-Spam Perspective 174

Responsible Email 175
Six Email Resolutions 176
The Append Issue 177

Problems With Email 179
Filtering Problems 179
You've Got Bogus Email 180

Email Precautions 181
Let's Test Again 182
Use the Right Software 182
Know Your Audience 184

9: TOOLS, SEALS, TECHNIQUES 189

Free Assistance 189
Commercial Privacy Products 190
PrivacyRight 190
IDcide 191
Watchfire 191
Zero Knowledge Systems 192
Privacy Council 192
Platform for Privacy Preferences Project 193
P3P in Internet Explorer 6 194

Other P3P Software 196
P3P in Practice 197
P3P Action Plan 199
Privacy Statements and P3P 200
Privacy Seals *201*
How Privacy Seals Work 201
TRUSTe 203
BBBOnLine 204
Email Privacy Technology *204*
Trusted Senders? 205

10: SUMMING UP 211

Great Exposure *211*
The Blame Game *212*
Final Checklist *215*

SOURCES 219

Model Privacy Statements and Policy Generators . *219*
Privacy Principles *219*
Privacy Laws *220*
Privacy Tools *220*
Privacy and Online Organizations *221*
European Union and International *221*
Agencies in E.U. and other countries *222*
General Security & Data Protection Links *223*
Recommended Reading *224*

ACKNOWLEDGMENTS

I don't know about other writers, but this is one part of the book I really enjoy writing, and not just because it means the book is finished. This is where I get to thank those whose words of encouragement and wisdom helped make the book a reality.

In many ways, a book like this is a rich brew of other people's ideas and observations, distilled by the author, with a few of his own ingredients stirred in for good measure. My esteemed colleagues at ePrivacy Group will certainly recognize in these pages points they have made and insights they have graciously shared. Many are attributed in the text, but some are already so ingrained in our "group think" that I am unaware of their precise origins. Needless to say, I owe a huge debt of personal and professional gratitude to the following gentlemen, whom I am proud to count as friends as well as co-workers: Vincent Schiavone, David Brussin, Michael Miora, James Koenig, Terry Pittman, Ray Everett-Church. I feel particularly privileged to count one special person as friend, co-worker, and brother. Thanks Mike.

I don't know if there is a good woman behind every good man, but I do know there are several good women behind this book and its author. For inspiration and support, no man could ask for more than I have in Chey, whose own example as an author rekindled my determination to put on paper what I had talked about for so long. For inspiration and editing, no son could ask for a better mother than mine. Dorothy's love of the language and her knowledge of Fowler made my original words considerably more effective and much less of a chore for you to read. For the inspiration of good news I must acknowledge Erin, who supplied me with so much of it during the writing of this book. Thanks daughter.

Finally, let me make it clear that the opinions expressed in this book are mine alone, and do not necessarily reflect the views of my employer or my publisher. Furthermore, any errors or inaccuracies you find within these pages are also mine alone, and I apologize for them in advance. If you point them out to me, at scobb@cobb.com, I would be most grateful. In the next edition I could be acknowledging you as well.

INTRODUCTION

The goal of this book is to help businesses and their employees learn what they need to know about privacy as it relates to company Web sites and email. Most businesses today operate at least one Web site; some large companies may have dozens of sites. Most Web sites come into contact with information that is considered personal by the people to whom it relates. Most of today's business also make use of email, to communicate with customers, both current and prospective. Most people who have email addresses consider them to be in some way private, and therefore to be treated with respect.

Many people today are very sensitive about how their personal information is handled. This sensitivity is reflected in recent laws and lawsuits, as well a media coverage and opinion polls, all of which imply that violating personal privacy has negative consequences. For businesses, these negative consequences can include lost revenue, reduced customer and investor confidence, burdensome government oversight and intervention, hefty fines, and possibly jail time.

Much of the current concern about privacy can be attributed to the increased ability of companies, governments, and even individuals, to collect, collate, and disseminate information digitally, as data. Some of that data is *personally identifiable information*, or PII. In other words, it is data that relates to a person who can be identified from the data, the *data subject*.

The Internet and the World Wide Web have been on the cutting edge of an enormous increase in the collection, processing, and distribution of PII by businesses. Unfortunately, technology is not perfect, and neither are its users. When a business handles PII, not only is the privacy of data subjects at risk, but so is the business itself. The goal of this book is to help your company minimize that risk, especially in the context of operating a Web site and sending email, thereby avoiding the unpleasant consequences that can arise from the inappropriate handling of personally identifiable data.

Is This Book for You?

This book is for anyone who works with, or is planning to work with, Web sites and personal information. It is also written for anyone who manages people who work with Web sites and personal information. That includes:

■ Web site managers, Webmasters, Web content managers

■ Employees who design and code Web sites

■ Sales and marketing managers and their staff

■ Any employee who handles personally identifiable data

■ Corporate counsel and corporate compliance officers

■ CEOs, CIOs, CTOs, CSOs, and CPOs

A wide range of people to be sure, but privacy encompasses many aspects of a business, as does email and Web site technology. In fact, Web sites and email are often the focal point for privacy concerns within a company, a logical place to start for the business that wants to get on top of this rapidly emerging issue. And while I cannot guarantee that all persons in all of the above categories will like what they read here, this book is written so that, regardless of which category you are in, what I say should make sense to you.

What This Book Is Not

I want you to be happy with your decision to purchase this book, but you won't be if it fails to meet your expectations. Allow me to further refine those expectations by telling you three things that this book does not do:

1. Provide consumer privacy education. This is not the book you buy to help you protect your privacy while surfing the Web. That book has been written already and a colleague of mine, Ray Everett-Church is the coauthor. The book is *Internet Privacy for Dummies*. Don't be insulted or misled by the title—I have a lot of respect for "Dummies" books, particularly since my wife wrote *Network Security for Dummies*.

2. Detail the reasons why citizens are, or should be, concerned about privacy. Although I describe, in broad terms, the background to consumer privacy concerns, the best book dedicated to that task is undoubtedly Simson Garfinkel's *Database Nation*. Although I don't always agree with Simson, we have had some very interesting conversations over the years and I have a great deal of respect for his scholarship and sincerity. In my opinion, *Database Nation* is required reading if you are planning to do some serious thinking about privacy for business today.

3. Detail the configuration of Web servers and browsers for maximum security. This task has been undertaken by a number of books. Simson's *Web Security and Commerce* is a good place to start. Information about specific Web software is available in more specialized titles, such as *IIS Security*, written by one of my former coauthors, Marty Jost, together with my brother, Mike Cobb.

Thank You

At this point, with your expectations suitably adjusted, it only remains for me to thank you for choosing this book to help you answer your questions about privacy for business. Let us proceed — it's time to get down to the business of privacy.

Stephen Cobb

CHAPTER ONE

PRIVACY AND BUSINESS TODAY

010101101110011011111010010111001010101011011011

2

"Over 80 percent of people surveyed by Harris said that they would completely stop doing business with a company that had misused customer information."

—*The Guardian*, May 2, 2002

1: Privacy and Business Today

Privacy is currently a subject of great concern to many consumers. You probably know this already—you are reading this book—but the point is worth emphasizing. No business today can claim ignorance of the importance of privacy as a concern among consumers, a concern that can have significant business impacts, from increased costs to revenues lost, from brand dilution to stock price depression. Every company that wants to interact with customers via the Internet should know that privacy concerns are the primary impediment to such interaction. In June of 2002, Jupiter Media Metrix calculated that as much as $24.5 billion worth of online sales will be lost by 2006 because Web sites are not addressing consumer fears about privacy and security. The effectiveness of email for consumer communication is threatened by the staggering volume of unwanted commercial email, or spam, which is regarded by many consumers as an invasion of privacy. More than three-quarters of online consumers surveyed in 2002 said that they delete unsolicited commercial emails without reading them. In this chapter I put today's privacy concerns in perspective and relate them to business Web sites and email practices.

Privacy Today

If you were to ask me what is the single most important thing that businesses need to "get" about privacy right now, I would say: the way customers feel. Most of the privacy challenges that businesses face today are driven by consumer sentiment about privacy and the high level of attention afforded that sentiment by the press, the lawyers, the lawmakers, and the regulators. Any company that is accused of violating consumer privacy, however inadvertently, will soon find this out. As I will explain in detail in Chapter 7, the right response to such accusations can be as critical as the steps you take to prevent them. But I can assure you right now that "We had no idea people would be so upset" is not an option.

When I conduct privacy seminars for businesses, one of the first slides I present is a collage of magazine covers collected over the last few years. They include both business and consumer publications and all of them feature privacy as the cover story. Here are some of the headlines:

- *PC Magazine*: Privacy War

- *CIO Magazine*: Are Your Medical Secrets Safe?

- *U.S. News & World Report*: The Dark Side of the Internet

- *TIME*: How To Protect Your Privacy Online

- *Red Herring*: Privacy—Why It Will Shape Ecommerce In 2001

- *Business 2.0*: Who Can You Trust?

- *Smart Business*: You're Being Watched!

- *Darwin*: Privacy Showdown

- *Popular Science*: All Eyes Are on You

- *Information Week*: Paranoia—Customers Worry About Misuse of Their Data. Maybe You Should Too

These articles reflect genuine concerns. When the Wall Street Journal and NBC conducted a telephone poll of more than 2,000 adults at the end of 1999 and asked them what they feared most in the coming century, "loss of personal privacy" topped the list; cited as the number one concern by 29 percent of respondents, well ahead of overpopulation, acts of terrorism, and racism. This concern is particularly acute with respect to the Internet; for example, a survey in June of 2002 by Jupiter Media Metrix found that almost 70 percent of U.S. consumers worry that their privacy is at risk online. This is not just a vague sentiment. A Harris survey in February of 2002 revealed the top three privacy concerns of consumers to be that:

(a) their information would be provided to other firms without their permission,

(b) their transactions may not be secure, and

(c) hackers could steal their personal information.

These findings are not just important for Web-based companies. If yours is a "clicks-and-mortar" company, one that combines Web operations with traditional business premises, you should note that, in the same Harris survey, over 80 percent of the respondents said that they would "completely stop doing business with a company that had misused customer information." In other words, as Jupiter analysts have pointed out:

"With poor online privacy practices, many companies will experience negative effects not only on their online sales over the next several years, but also on off-line sales that shift to more privacy-sensitive competitors."

Privacy and Terrorism: While the tragic events of September 11, 2001, have undoubtedly increased anxiety over terrorism, there is no indication that people are any less concerned about privacy. Indeed, many of the government's responses to 9/11 involve increases in surveillance; and while some of these responses have a sound strategic basis, others have heightened fears about the loss of personal privacy. The overall effect of 9/11 on privacy has been to push it even further up the public agenda. That may be a good thing, because what many consumers and businesses currently point to as privacy problems are in fact privacy paradoxes, issues about which we have not yet, as a society, thought enough to frame the debate, let alone take sides.

Privacy Questions

So why is privacy such a hot issue today? Is it just media hype? Surely the notion of privacy has been around for a long time? These are legitimate questions. The easiest to answer is the one about media hype, because the surveys quoted earlier are only a few of many that indicate pretty much the same thing: People fear their privacy is at risk. While studies have shown that this fear does not always prevent consumers from sharing personal information with companies, studies also show that privacy concerns are getting more, not less pervasive. At the same, evidence of a positive response to respect for privacy is getting stronger.

To understand the causes of current concerns about privacy, think of them as the shock waves and fallout from an unprecedented information technology explosion. There are clear parallels to this phenomenon in the history of other technologies. Consider the internal combustion engine or nuclear energy. An early phase of great enthusiasm was accompanied by rapid and widespread adoption—during which any doubts and reservations were swept aside by acclaim for the technology's benefits—eventually leading to the drawbacks and downsides becoming so obvious as to be undeniable.

During the last twenty years we witnessed an unprecedented increase in the ability of companies, governments, and individuals, to collect, collate, and disseminate information. This clearly resulted in enormous consumer and social benefits. Information technology enabled, largely through productivity gains, many years of strong economic growth accompanied by low inflation and full employment. But what about the side effects? For example, if you tell me your name there is a good chance I can figure out, within minutes, where you live, what your house looks like and how much it is worth. I will know how to get there, what shops and restaurants are nearby, plus where you work and what your email address is. The really scary part is that I can do that, in most cases, with just a Web browser and an Internet connection, no special service or database access fee required.

What can be done with more resources? I can take a name and address list to a specialist and get it analyzed, enhanced, and appended. The analysis does things like determine gender and ethnicity, while the enhancement can add age, number of persons in household, head of household's name and age, estimated household income, single or multifamily dwelling, length of residence, owner or renter status, bank card in household, marital status, number of adults, presence of children. A process known as appending can add things to your data like time zone, latitude and longitude of the five digit ZIP code, county name, and congressional district. All of this is automated and thousands of records can be processed in minutes. A different service can figure out a person's email address at work, in case I have a list of names without email addresses.

Some people have portrayed this sort of technology as inherently sinister, but that misses the point raised earlier: the tension between what is personal and what is public has been around for a long time. With the possible exception of a few hermits and outlaws, people have always lived their lives as known entities; where they lived and worked and shopped, and what they bought when they shopped, were all facts known to at least a few other people.

Privacy Perspective: About ten years ago my family and I lived for several years in a village in Scotland which, in many ways, exemplified the much sought-after ideal of a caring and supportive community. We soon learned that the sharing of personal information was not only essential to the functioning of such a community, it was also both desirable and unavoidable. For example, one's state of health was widely known—the doctor made house calls and everyone could see at whose house he was calling. If things were serious there might be very specific prayers for you in church on Sunday, followed by offers of care and assistance.

What is different today is the way in which information technology has transformed information. Consider "access to public records." Information technology fundamentally alters the meaning of this term because of what IT does to the speed and distance factors that govern accessibility. One of my favorite movies is *Chinatown*, in which Jack Nicholson plays a private detective who uses public records to figure out a huge property scam. If you know the movie you know it also takes him several days, two fistfights, and at least one illegal act. Obviously, the word "access" means one thing when you have to go down to the local hall of records, find the right piece of paper and literally rip it off; quite another if it only takes few keystrokes in the comfort of your home.

The transformation of information by technology is further amplified when you multiply the number of sources that can be tapped simultaneously in this way. While one piece of personal information alone may not be of much value, adding a second piece often more than doubles its value. For example, you may be able to use one piece to leverage another. Consider your mother's maiden name. If someone knows that, they may be able to get at a lot of other information (many institutions use this name as a form of password—even though it is a lot easier to find someone's mother's maiden name now there are so many genealogy sites on the Web). If you have worked in computer security you will be familiar with the phenomenon that is sometimes referred to as "incremental information leveraging." An attacker will sift through company garbage for inside information such as internal phone directories. Armed with one of these, an attacker can then "social engineer" a network password from an employee by pretending to be someone from technical support. As more and more information makes its way onto the Web or is transmitted via email, this type of attack becomes much easier to execute, with less risk of detection.

A very similar mix of analogue and digital techniques is employed by identity thieves, who can parlay a few details about a person into a lot of money, typically in the form of unpaid credit card bills in the name of the person whose identity they have stolen (see Figure 1-1). Identity theft has been called the fastest growing crime in America and it is clearly one of the main reasons that today's consumers are so concerned about how their personal information is handled.

Five years ago I heard a chilling presentation about identity theft at the annual DefCon hacker convention in Las Vegas, delivered by a John Q. Newman, author of *Identity Theft*. His talk related an interview with a man from England who makes his living stealing American identities. Every year this man flies over to the United States armed with personal information about his intended victims that he has harvested from Web sites. By combining this information with data from consumer credit reports, plus a basic knowledge of financial systems and a natural aptitude for social engineering, this man is able to illegally obtain goods, services, bank accounts, and credit cards that he then converts into cash to the tune of $40,000 or more before going back to England. Each summer he leaves behind a handful of victims who may take years to recover from this assault. There will be more about identity theft in Chapter 2.

What is Web Privacy?

High levels of concern over privacy have, as you might expect, fueled debate about the definition of the word itself. The finer details of the debate are beyond the scope of this book but there is a good working definition for people who have to deal with privacy in a Web context, provided by the Electronic Privacy Information Center:

"the right of individuals to control the collection, use, and dissemination of personal information that is held by others." (EPIC: www.epic.org)

Web privacy is thus the right of individuals to control the collection, use, and dissemination of personal information that is held by Web sites. In broader terms, Web privacy also means making sure that your Web site's handling of personally identifiable information complies with a wide range of applicable laws, industry standards, and business best practices. In short, if it is personally identifiable information, your Web site and your company need to "Handle With Care." Failure to do so could result in problems ranging from angry customers and lost business to fines and imprisonment (you can read a lot more about the negative consequences of privacy problems in Chapter 2).

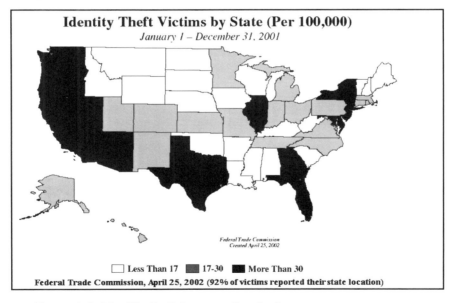

Figure 1-1: Identity theft is spreading fast

Data Ownership

When you are responsible for a business Web site it is natural to think in terms of *you* versus *them*—where *them* is anyone who tries to compromise the confidentiality, integrity, or availability of *your* data. In fact, it is unlikely that all the data handled by your Web site actually belongs to you. The people who visit your site will generate or supply data, some of which can be said to belong to them and not you. This might be data that you actively request—for example, information needed to complete an online order form—but it could also be passive data, such as logs showing who visited the site and what pages they viewed.

Some of the people to whom this data relates may consider it private information—that is, they may think that they have a right to determine how it is used and by whom. Plus you may have a legal obligation to allow people to review and make changes to data pertaining to them that your Web site collects, stores, or processes. The Children's Online Privacy Protection Act contains such a provision, and a case settled in August of 2002 requires one of the Internet's largest ad companies, DoubleClick, to disclose to Web users the information it compiles on them in order to customize the selection of ads at some of the Web's largest commercial sites.

Non-public Web sites: Some Web sites may be exempt from privacy requirements because they are not freely accessible to the general public. Access to such sites typically is limited to a group of people, such as employees, who use the Web site for access to company information. A non-public Web site controls all access of any kind, effectively acting like an internal or intranet web site. Such sites may not be subject to some of the legal disclosure requirements that apply to public Web sites. When this distinction arises in later chapters, the terms **public Web site** and **non-public Web site** will be used in this way to make the distinction clear .

Common sense says you should use reasonable security measures to protect the confidentiality of any information relating to individuals that your Web site handles, but some privacy legislation has made such security mandatory. For example, if your company is involved in financial services you probably know that the Gramm-Leach-Bliley Act holds the board of directors responsible for information security (specifically, for "approving and overseeing the development, implementation, and maintenance of the institution's efforts to ensure the security and confidentiality of customer information and protect against any anticipated threats or hazards to the security or integrity of such information"). The board is also responsible for protection against unauthorized access to or use of such information that could result in substantial harm or inconvenience to any customer.

Privacy Acronyms

Like any other subject, privacy has its own acronyms. As I mentioned in the Introduction, the acronym PII is commonly used for "Personally Identifiable Information." You may find the term defined differently in different places, but the following definition is not only typical, it is particularly relevant since it comes from a government ruling in a privacy case involving a business Web site: "PII is individually identifiable information from or about an individual consumer including, but not limited to:

(a) a first and last name;

(b) a home or other physical address, including street name and name of city or town;

(c) an email address or other online contact information, such as an instant messaging user identifier or a screen name that reveals an individual's email address;

(d) a telephone number;

(e) a social security number;

(f) an Internet Protocol (IP) address or host name that identifies an individual consumer;

(g) a persistent identifier, such as a customer number held in a "cookie" or processor serial number, that is combined with other available data that identifies an individual consumer; or

(h) any information that is combined with (a) through (g) above."

If this strikes you as a pretty broad definition, you probably need to expand your privacy horizon, because some privacy advocates will tell you this does not go far enough. In its Data Protection Directive, discussed in Chapter 5, the European Union highlights several other aspects of PII, including any identification number assigned to a person, or one or more factors specific to "physical, physiological, mental, economic, cultural or social identity."

To put this in perspective you need to realize that "personally identifiable information" is a relative concept. The context in which information appears can be critical. Consider this piece of information: jprz268@msn.com. This doesn't look very personal. You could say it reveals nothing, but connect it to other pieces of information and it can be both personal and revealing. What if it appears in a list of email addresses belonging to people who have expressed an interest in Viagra? If you happen to know who uses the email address jprz268@msn.com, that is immediately revealing. If jprz268@msn.com appears as the sender of an email message that contains illegal information, then law enforcement may well be able to find out who is using it, making it a very personally identifiable piece of information.

Another way to focus on the meaning of PII is to look at a group of people, such as "all people in the county." For most counties in most countries, this is not a piece of personally identifiable information. The statement that "ten percent of the residents of Cobb County use marijuana" is not revealing any PII. A list of how many people in each age group in Cobb County take antidepressants is probably not PII either. But what if there was only one person in one of the age groups? In that case a group definition would constitute PII. Improbable perhaps, but think about "all men in the county over ninety." In some counties this might be one person, who is thus identified without the use of his name. Adding a second and third factor, such as gender and age, can turn a broad category into a personal identifier. In fact, marketing experts and law enforcement alike have developed considerable skill at identifying specific individuals by overlaying several pieces of nonspecific data.

Such distinctions are far from academic, although some academics have a keen interest in them, particularly when the data is health-related. By analyzing large accumulations of health data, medical researchers can discover remarkable and potentially lifesaving facts. However, the privacy implications of giving researchers access to large amounts of health data are enormous. One strategy is to "de-identify" the data, that is, strip it of any information that could enable someone to identify the individuals to whom it refers. The rules for doing this must take into account the relative nature of PII. For example, there are guidelines for the de-identification of medical data in the rules implementing the Health Insurance

Portability and Accountability Act (known as HIPAA and discussed in detail in Chapter 4). If you read the ninety pages of densely-packed, three-column Federal Register text that constitute the final version of the HIPAA Privacy Rule, you will see that exceptions had to be made for certain ZIP codes when de-identifying data (see Figure 1-2). There are several variations on PII, notably PIMI, PMI, PHI, PMI and IIHI, all of which may be found in discussions of health information privacy and in legislation such as HIPAA. Here's what each one stands for:

PIMI: Personally Identifiable Medical Information

PMI: Personal Medical Information

PHI: Protected Health Information

IIHI: Individually Identifiable Health Information

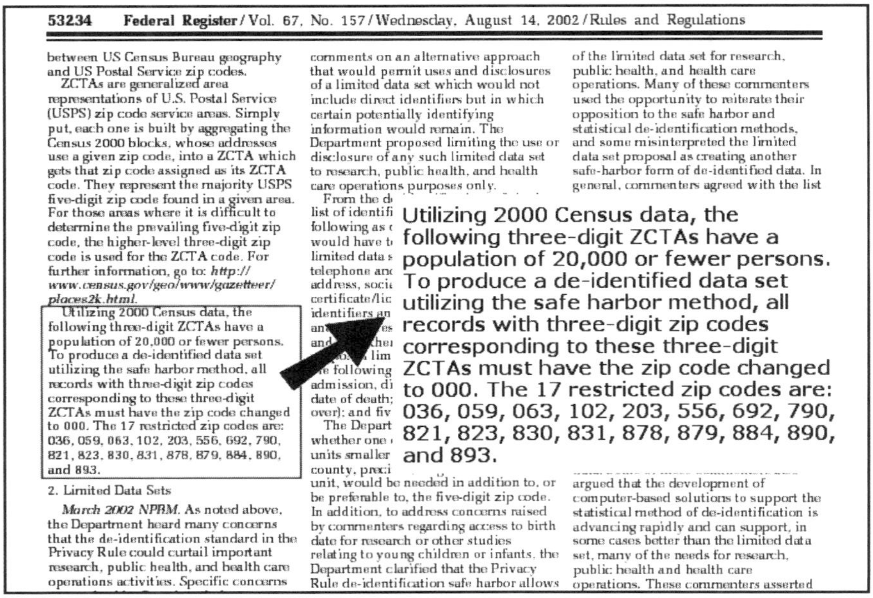

53234   Federal Register/Vol. 67, No. 157/Wednesday, August 14, 2002/Rules and Regulations

between U.S Census Bureau geography and US Postal Service zip codes.

ZCTAs are generalized area representations of U.S. Postal Service (USPS) zip code service areas. Simply put, each one is built by aggregating the Census 2000 blocks, whose addresses use a given zip code, into a ZCTA which gets that zip code assigned as its ZCTA code. They represent the majority USPS five-digit zip code found in a given area. For those areas where it is difficult to determine the prevailing five-digit zip code, the higher-level three-digit zip code is used for the ZCTA code. For further information, go to: *http://www.census.gov/geo/www/gazetteer/places2k.html*.

Utilizing 2000 Census data, the following three-digit ZCTAs have a population of 20,000 or fewer persons. To produce a de-identified data set utilizing the safe harbor method, all records with three-digit zip codes corresponding to these three-digit ZCTAs must have the zip code changed to 000. The 17 restricted zip codes are: 036, 059, 063, 102, 203, 556, 692, 790, 821, 823, 830, 831, 878, 879, 884, 890, and 893.

2. Limited Data Sets

March 2002 NPRM. As noted above, the Department heard many concerns that the de-identification standard in the Privacy Rule could curtail important research, public health, and health care operations activities. Specific concerns

comments on an alternative approach that would permit uses and disclosures of a limited data set which would not include direct identifiers but in which certain potentially identifying information would remain. The Department proposed limiting the use or disclosure of any such limited data set to research, public health, and health care operations purposes only.

From the d

list of identifi

following as c

would have t

limited data s

telephone and

address, socia

certificate/lic

identifiers an

an   es

and   he

following

admission, di

date of death;

over); and fiv

The Depart

whether one c

units smaller

county, preci

unit, would be needed in addition to, or be preferable to, the five-digit zip code. In addition, to address concerns raised by commenters regarding access to birth date for research or other studies relating to young children or infants, the Department clarified that the Privacy Rule de-identification safe harbor allows

of the limited data set for research, public health, and health care operations. Many of these commenters used the opportunity to reiterate their opposition to the safe harbor and statistical de-identification methods, and some misinterpreted the limited data set proposal as creating another safe-harbor form of de-identified data. In general, commenters agreed with the list

Utilizing 2000 Census data, the following three-digit ZCTAs have a population of 20,000 or fewer persons. To produce a de-identified data set utilizing the safe harbor method, all records with three-digit zip codes corresponding to these three-digit ZCTAs must have the zip code changed to 000. The 17 restricted zip codes are: 036, 059, 063, 102, 203, 556, 692, 790, 821, 823, 830, 831, 878, 879, 884, 890, and 893.

argued that the development of computer-based solutions to support the statistical method of de-identification is advancing rapidly and can support, in some cases better than the limited data set, many of the needs for research, public health and health care operations. These commenters asserted

Figure 1-2 ZIP codes and HIPAA in the Federal Register

Why so many similar and overlapping privacy acronyms? Because data privacy is still an emerging topic, the language of which is still evolving. Although PII, PHI, and IIHI are now fairly well-established in privacy circles, you can help avoid confusion and false assumptions if you explain privacy acronyms whenever you use them.

Legal Angles

Many countries have determined that the privacy of PII is important enough to merit legal protection. In some, that legal protection takes the form of broad privacy legislation which applies to almost all personal data in almost every situation. In other countries, notably the United States, the legislated protection of privacy is piecemeal, applying only to certain information in certain circumstances. For example, the privacy of your video rental records is specifically protected by the Video Privacy Protection Act (created in 1989, shortly after newspapers published a list of movies rented by Supreme Court nominee Robert Bork—presumably passed in a hurry by politicians concerned that their movie choices might otherwise see the light of day).

Note that legislation is not the only way to provide legal protection for PII. A number of experts have argued that Americans enjoy extensive privacy protection under tort law. In other words, citizens have a right to sue for damages if they think they have suffered harm due to an invasion of their privacy. This position is extensively documented in a report prepared by Privacilla.org, a non-profit organization that describes itself as "Your source for privacy policy from a free-market, pro-technology perspective." Here is the conclusion of the report:

> "The privacy torts provide baseline privacy protections, below which no company or individual may go. They are not limited to any type of information or medium. They cover all information, including medical and financial information, and they apply equally to communications on or off the Internet."

A similar claim is articulated by the U.S. Department of Commerce in a paper titled "Damages for Breaches of Privacy, Legal Authorizations and Mergers and Takeovers in U.S. Law." The paper was prepared in 2000, as part of the negotiations between the United States and the European Union over data protection and something called Safe Harbor, a topic covered in more detail in Chapter 5. The goal of the negotiations was to assure Europeans that America can be a safe place for personal data despite the fact that the legal protections in America are not based on the broad legislated protection of data privacy to which Europeans have become accustomed. The paper asserts that:

> "The right to recover damages for invasion of personal privacy is well established under U.S. common law."

On the issue of damages, the paper concludes that invasions of privacy in the United States give injured parties the right to recover damages for any harm to their interest in privacy that results from the invasion, plus any mental distress proved to have been suffered, if it is of a kind that normally results from such an invasion. There may also be special damages of which the invasion is a legal cause (for an example of this, consider what happened when the *National Inquirer* breached the medical privacy of singer Tammy Wynette and reported that she needed a liver transplant — she suffered a loss of revenue due to cancelled bookings).

Privacy Promises: Recently, a completely different legal angle has been used to enforce what are being referred to as "privacy promises." If a company promises its customers that it will protect the privacy of their information and then fails to keep that promise, a charge of deceptive business practice maybe forthcoming, either from the Federal Trade Commission or any number of state business regulators. There is more about privacy cases of this type in Chapters 2 and 4.

While a detailed discussion of legal theory is beyond the scope of this book, knowing the lay of the land will help because privacy legislation and privacy litigation make a big difference to your company's responsibilities as a Web site operator or sender of email. Based on such parameters as intended audience, physical location, and type of content, your Web site may be subject to specific legislated privacy requirements. In addition, your company has underlying and much less specific legal obligations with respect to people's privacy, as well as other general legal obligations. Chapter 4 addresses U.S. legal requirements in more detail and Chapter 5 describes the privacy challenges that arise from the global nature of the World Wide Web.

Standard Legal Disclaimer: At point I should reiterate the standard legal disclaimer that says: "The information contained in this book is for general guidance only. The application and impact of laws can vary widely based on the specific facts involved. Accordingly, the information in this book is provided with the understanding that the author and publisher are not herein engaged in rendering legal, or other professional advice and services. As such, it should not be used as a substitute for consultation with professional legal or other advisers."

Privacy Positives

Hopefully, most commercial Web site operators will regard the legal requirements of privacy as a baseline, a minimum standard that they will want to exceed in the interests of good business. Privacy as a positive business differentiator is certainly a theme you will find repeated throughout this book. While there will be a lot of talk about the potential for negative consequences from what is commonly referred to as a *privacy incident* or a *privacy breach*, privacy can also be defined in a positive way. For example, on the right of Figure 1-3 you can see a "privacy seal" displayed on a Web site.

Figure 1-3: An example of a Web privacy seal

This seal represents a form of self-regulation among Web site operators—the seal can be displayed only by sites that meet or exceed a voluntary, self-imposed set of privacy standards. One powerful indicator of privacy's importance to Web users is the fact that within three years of its launch, the TRUSTe seal was the most clicked symbol on the Web, way ahead of second-place Microsoft and registering more impressions than Yahoo!, Amazon, and eBay combined. All major Web portals display the seal, and it can be found on 15 of the 20 most popular Web sites and on more than half of the top 100 sites.

Obviously, there are costs associated with using such programs, but the risk of negative legal and business impacts arising from a privacy breach makes risk mitigation a worthwhile investment for many companies. Chapter 9 has more about Web site privacy seals as well as Web privacy tools and technologies that are being developed to aid in risk mitigation. In Chapter 10 the business case for Web privacy will be stated in more detail.

Privacy Paradoxes

Of all the tasks involved in making sure that your Web site and email communications are an asset to your organization and not a liability, privacy is probably the most mentally challenging. When you start to come to grips with privacy issues, you can quickly find yourself wondering why it seems to be such difficult work. Hopefully, this section will help you understand why Web privacy is so difficult, and it will give you a framework for dealing with some of the tough decisions that you, or someone in your organization, will have to make about privacy.

Privacy is a formidable challenge because nobody yet understands exactly what privacy means in today's highly interconnected, heavily computerized, data-dependent world. About the best we can say is that privacy in the information age is a work in progress. In the same way that environmental risks continue to emerge as the dark side of the industrial/technological age, emerging privacy risks have been cast as the dark side of the information age.

Whether or not you agree with that assessment, it is indisputable that many people see databases and computer networks as a threat to their personal privacy. Thus, to the extent that your business depends on access to, or makes use of, personal information, you will want to provide reassurances to those who need them, regarding the handling and protection of their personal information.

On the other hand, a lot of people enjoy considerable commercial benefits from information technology, many of which depend upon the sharing of personal information. A widely cited example is consumer credit, rapid and widespread access to which has been made possible by the sharing of information about people's accounts and payment histories.

Other examples are personalized service, special offers, and loyalty programs. When I stay at my preferred hotel chain, for example, I automatically receive expedited check-in, a free room upgrade, and a bottle of wine. Naturally, I choose to stay at this hotel chain whenever I can. The same principles can be seen at work in frequent traveler mileage programs operated by airlines.

Such personalized brand loyalty programs are possible only when customers are willing to trust companies with private information, such as travel plans and personal preferences (typically through use of an assigned customer number). If my preferred company were to betray my trust — for example, by selling my preferences without my permission to a marketing company, which then used them to pester me with sales calls — chances are it would cease to be my preferred company.

Wherever consumers see their trust abused, or perceive a lack of trustworthiness in those to whom they entrust personal information, they usually show reluctance in sharing personal information. In the context of the Web, and email this is reflected in consumers' reluctance to provide credit card information to Web sites, which surveys have consistently linked to doubts about the ability of Web sites to keep such personal data secure. The first privacy paradox can thus be stated as *a reluctance to divulge personal information, despite a desire for personalized products and services.*

The second privacy paradox concerns the *ownership* of information. Consider your company's customer list, the names and addresses of people who have purchased your products or services. Traditionally, businesses consider such information to be the property of the business. Indeed, customer data can be a valuable business asset, particularly if it includes purchase histories, buying habits, personal preferences, and similar information. You only have to imagine what a competitor could do with such data to understand that it merits the protection of strong security measures, such as access control and encryption. However, your company's ownership of this data is, in many ways, shared with the people to whom it relates—and some of this sharing is prescribed by law.

Privacy Target: Do not underestimate how upset some visitors to your Web site can become if they think you have done, or have even thought about doing, anything that might amount to an invasion of their privacy. Many Web site defacement and Denial of Service (DoS) attacks are motivated by an attacker's feelings of righteous indignation. While such attacks can never be justified, taking steps to avoid becoming a target makes sense, particularly when those steps, such as posting and abiding by a comprehensive privacy statement, already make sense from a business perspective.

Consider your bank: it has both a right and a duty to know how much money you have in your account, but a number of laws limit how, and with whom, the bank can share this information. On the one hand, your bank is prohibited from sharing the information with you, unless it takes reasonable steps to assure that you are, in fact, you—a challenge that operators of banking Web sites will recognize.

On the other hand, the bank can tell anyone it likes how much money you have in your account, if that data is either aggregated or "de-identified" (stripped of identifying data). Your bank can share detailed and fully identified information about you with another company, such as a stock brokerage or insurance affiliate *if* it has your permission to do so.

Yet your permission is not required for the bank to reveal certain information about your account to the government (some deposits and withdrawals must be reported under various laws relating to money laundering, tax evasion, and terrorism). The bank is also required to tell you what information it maintains about you and give you an opportunity to correct any errors within that information.

So the second privacy paradox is this: *a company's ownership of information about people, such as its customers, may not preclude their ownership of certain aspects or pieces of that information.* And the third privacy paradox is that *ownership of information about people may create an obligation to share some of that information, for example with government agencies or individuals identified by the data.*

The Europeans Have a Word for It: Instead of saying "the individual identified by the data" or "the person to whom the data refers," the Europeans use the term "data subject," which I find very convenient. You will find it used in this sense throughout the book.

The Privacy Landscape

Something else that will help you deal with privacy issues pertaining to your business use of the Internet is a clear picture of the *privacy landscape.* In the United States the privacy landscape is shaped by two main forces: marketers and privacy advocates.

The marketers want to use information about data subjects to sell more products—for example, to target data subjects with a specific message: "Dear Jane: We know you enjoy up-market shopping and staying in fine hotels, so you'll be happy to know that rates at our MegaMall Resort are 50 percent off this month." Use of data for marketing purposes can also mean analyzing large amounts of information to discover trends (urban couples with new babies tend to dine at home, so send them offers from restaurants that deliver—and send offers from more upscale eateries to certain zip codes, based on property values and median incomes).

Privacy advocates want greater legal restrictions on what companies can do with information about individuals. Many privacy advocates in the United States would like to establish a clear and general legal right of data privacy where none currently exists, so that individuals can know they have some control over how information about them is used, regardless of whatever new ways of using such information may be developed. A representative statement of this position can be found in the book *Database Nation*, by Simson Garfinkel:

"In these chapters, I've argued that the most effective solution for preventing the unwanted collection and disclosure of personal information is sweeping legislation designed to restore our right to privacy in this age of computers."

As you might expect, marketers and privacy advocates disagree a lot. For example, here is the conclusion drawn by Sonia Arrison in the study "Consumer Privacy: A Free Choice Approach," published by the Pacific Research Institute for Public Policy:

"New laws governing the collection of consumer information are not needed....Instead, new information restrictions would usurp consumer choice, drive up prices for consumers, and strangle business, especially small business, with red tape."

That people disagree about privacy is to be expected. The debate over what to do about privacy is intellectually challenging and you may find yourself drawn into it on a personal level. What you need to know from a business perspective is that the debate is far from academic.

Privacy advocates today act as unofficial privacy watchdogs. Their role in several landmark cases, cited in different chapters, has been significant. Major corporations have faced serious regulatory action involving Web site privacy issues, due in no small part to the advocacy of groups like the ACLU and EPIC (respectively, the American Civil Liberties Union and the Electronic Privacy Information Center). If the folks in your marketing department are the driving force behind your company Web site or email communications, take note: You may need to balance their perspective with the near certainty that any flagrant violation of what privacy advocates consider to be "fair information practices" will come to their attention, with potentially costly consequences.

As was noted at the beginning of this chapter, every major business and computer publication has run at least one cover story about privacy in the last two years. This means you will not be able deflect privacy-related criticism of simply by saying "I didn't know it was *that* important."

Privacy Policies and Statements

The widespread media coverage of privacy helps explains why, when you visit any Web site belonging to a well-known company, there's a good chance you will see a link on the home page that contains the word *privacy* (there is an example from IBM's Web site in Figure 1-4).

Figure 1-4 Corporate Web site privacy link (from ibm.com)

Such links invariably lead to a page stating the company's Web site privacy policies. There was an example of this earlier from IBM's Web site (Figure 1-3). The first task for a company getting to grips with Web site privacy is to make sure that all of the main pages on the company Web site have a link to a page about privacy.

The privacy page may be called a Privacy Statement or Privacy Notice. Some sites use the term Privacy Policy although, as I explain in Chapter 6, that might not be the best term to use in this context.

The Better Business Bureau, or BBB, is another well-known organization that provides a privacy seal. The BBB describes a good privacy notice as:

"easy to find, easy to read, and comprehensively explains all your online information practices."

In other words, a privacy notice or statement should be an integral part of your site's design. The creation of a privacy statement is covered in Chapter 6.

Note that a privacy notice should be posted even if your Web site does not collect or maintain any PII. For a start, visitors to your site don't know you are not collecting information about them unless you tell them. A privacy notice for such a site may not have a whole lot to say, but the fact that you have gone to the trouble of saying it may win you praise and deflect potential criticism. Furthermore, if you later decide to do things with your site that require the collection of information, having a privacy notice in place already will make it easier. You simply expand the existing notice — the necessary links are already in place.

Posting a privacy notice on your Web site is not just a matter of looking professional. Evidence from consumer surveys shows that people look for such statements when browsing at new sites, and people pay particular attention to them when shopping on the Web.

You may have seen some surveys suggesting that few consumers read privacy statements. This may well be true, but it does not mean they don't notice when a site doesn't have one. If the experience of sites that display a privacy seal is any indication, this extra attention to privacy is well rewarded. Surveys indicate that nine out of ten Web users actually mistrust privacy statements *unless* the site uses a third-party oversight program such as TRUSTe. (See Chapter 9 for more on how to get one for your Web site.)

What's Next?

Now that I have laid the basic groundwork, I want to give you a closer look at privacy problems that can arise from company Web sites and email operations. Chapter 2 describes privacy incidents that have shaped the privacy landscape for businesses, and the costs that incidents of this type can incur. Beginning in Chapter 3, I start to assemble the building blocks of business privacy solutions, starting with basic privacy principles. Chapter 4 examines how those principles are embodied in privacy laws, and what those laws imply for business Web sites and email. Because WWW stands for *World Wide* Web, Chapter 5 examines the international aspects of privacy for business. In Chapter 6, the task of creating privacy policy is described. The need for an overall business strategy with respect to privacy is addressed in Chapter 7, which also describes strategies for responding to privacy incidents. Chapter 8 focuses on privacy and email, while Chapter 9 looks at tools that are available to help with privacy tasks. In the final chapter, Chapter 10, there is a summing up, together with some of my thoughts about what all of this means for businesses and why good privacy practices are good for business.

Chapter Two

Privacy Incidents and Their Costs

010101101110011011111010010111001010101011011011

"Online retail sales would be approximately 24 percent higher in 2006 if consumers' fears about privacy and security were addressed effectively. With poor online privacy practices, many companies will experience negative effects not only on their online sales over the next several years, but also on off-line sales that shift to more privacy-sensitive competitors. Jupiter forecasts that as much as $24.5 billion in online sales will be lost by 2006, up from $5.5 billion in 2001." —*Online Privacy: Managing Complexity to Realize Marketing Benefits*, Jupiter Media Metrix (www.jmm.com).

2: PRIVACY INCIDENTS AND THEIR COSTS

In this chapter I describe the kind of Web privacy problems you want to avoid and the costs you can incur if you don't. Some are real cases, others are hypothetical. I want to give you an idea of the range of problems that can arise and the seriousness of their potential impacts on the business. The goal is to help you identify potential problems at your company and encourage you to take the appropriate steps to deal with them. This chapter should also prove helpful if you are trying to raise privacy awareness within your organization. Showing people real examples of what can go wrong is a proven strategy for encouraging them to trying harder to get things right.

Defining "Privacy Incident"

The first step to understanding privacy incidents is defining what they are. Consider this definition: a privacy-related event with potentially negative consequences. In fact, articles and presentations about privacy often use "privacy incident" as shorthand for "damaging privacy incident." Examples of such events include: hackers gaining unauthorized access to your Web site and stealing personal information about your customers; an employee using her authorized access to customer records to find sensitive information to sell to the press; your marketing department emailing sales literature to customers who asked not to receive such email; upper management deciding to make changes to the company's Web site privacy policy that result in widespread public criticism of the company.

Not all privacy incidents result from lapses in security. Some are violations of policy while others result from poor judgment. To define "privacy incident" in plain English: it has to do with privacy, and it's not good. In the specific context of Web privacy you might say: something's happened, it has to do with privacy and the Web site, and it's not good. This is undoubtedly what some employees at pharmaceutical giant Eli Lilly thought in June of 2001 when they found out that the email addresses of people who had registered on the company's prozac.com Web site — "Your Guide to Evaluating and Recovering from Depression"—had been publicly revealed due to an error in an email program written by the company's information services department.

You will find the Prozac Email Incident widely reported and discussed in privacy journals, but not because anyone wants to make an example out of this particular company. The simple fact is that the Prozac Email Incident was the first of its kind and so it has become the defining Web-related privacy incident: a programming error led to a privacy breach which drew public criticism and triggered a regulatory response. In many ways it was the privacy nightmare scenario, but that also means much can be learned from it, hopefully preventing future incidents of this type.

The Costs of a Privacy Incident

A privacy incident can cost a business in many different ways, from the number of person hours diverted to deal with the incident, to the loss of customers and brand value. This section discusses different types of cost, illustrating them with some real world examples.

Scrutiny and Glare

There may be a few people for whom there is some truth in the saying "There's no such thing as bad publicity," but don't try telling that to your CEO right before she has to take a call from a Washington Post reporter who wants to know why your company's Web site revealed the credit card numbers of several thousand customers. For businesses, there definitely *is* such a thing as bad publicity. Consumers tend to vote with their wallets and unless your company happens to have a monopoly, the media glare associated with bad news can rapidly impact the bottom line as customers switch to other suppliers.

Bad news can also have a cumulative effect. For example, less than six months after Eli Lilly reached a settlement with the Federal Trade Commission (FTC) regarding the aforementioned prozac.com privacy problem, the company was accused of another Prozac-related privacy violation. This second case involved samples of Prozac which were mailed to people in Florida, through a marketing deal involving—allegedly—the recipient's physician, the recipient's pharmacist, and Eli Lilly sales reps. The incident did not involve the Internet or the company Web site, but you can bet that reporters writing about this latest incident took the opportunity to remind people of the company's troubles with the FTC over the earlier Prozac-related privacy incident.

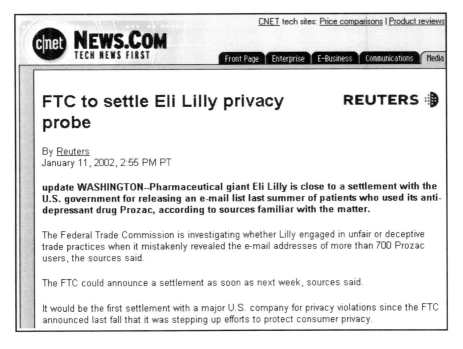

CNET tech sites: Price comparisons | Product reviews

NEWS.COM
TECH NEWS FIRST

Front Page | Enterprise | E-Business | Communications | Media

FTC to settle Eli Lilly privacy probe

REUTERS

By Reuters
January 11, 2002, 2:55 PM PT

update WASHINGTON--Pharmaceutical giant Eli Lilly is close to a settlement with the U.S. government for releasing an e-mail list last summer of patients who used its antidepressant drug Prozac, according to sources familiar with the matter.

The Federal Trade Commission is investigating whether Lilly engaged in unfair or deceptive trade practices when it mistakenly revealed the e-mail addresses of more than 700 Prozac users, the sources said.

The FTC could announce a settlement as soon as next week, sources said.

It would be the first settlement with a major U.S. company for privacy violations since the FTC announced last fall that it was stepping up efforts to protect consumer privacy.

Figure 2-1 Eli Lilly settlement reported on CNET

To understand the costs of a privacy incident in general, and the costs of scrutiny in particular, it might help to think of a rock thrown into a pond. First, there is a large initial splash at the point of entry. In the Prozac Email Incident, this was the message hitting the in-baskets of the hundreds of recipients, each of whom could see the email address of the other people who got the same revealing message. From the initial splash, waves emanate in concentric circles, the first wave being a call to the American Civil Liberties Union (ACLU). This was followed by the ACLU taking the matter to the FTC, then the press coverage of the incident and the ACLU's involvement. When the FTC decided to pursue the matter there was more press.

Eventually the waves spread out across the entire pond and start rippling back. This is the deployment of Eli Lilly resources to respond, first to internal personnel, then to the press, then to the FTC. Employees had to be interviewed to find out what happened. Documents had to be assembled ready to submit to the FTC investigators. Decisions had to be made about how to respond, what documents to submit and which to hold back. Legal counsel had to be consulted at all stages of the response process. Probably there were several rounds of document requests from the FTC as it framed its complaint (published on the FTC web site, and quoted later in this chapter). Eventually, a settlement is negotiated, which brings more headlines (see Figure 2-1).

Settlement Costs

Depending on the relative size of the rock and the pond into which it is pitched, the waves can keep going for some time. The original Prozac Email Incident occurred at the end of June, 2001. In January of 2002, Eli Lilly agreed to settle the FTC charges. In doing so, the company did not have to admit any violations of the law, but it did have to accept a series of requirements set out by the FTC, including close oversight of certain internal and external activities. Some of the requirements extend twenty years into the future and failure to meet them could result in fines, further actions, and an extension of the period of compliance beyond twenty years. The Sources section at the end of the book has more about what the FTC required, but the following is a short summary:

■ Create and maintain an information security program that identifies, and defends against, all internal and external security risks to personal information from or about consumers, including any risks due to lack of training.

- Complete a written review of the security program within 90 days of the agreement, and every year after that.

- Make available to the FTC all reports, studies, reviews, audits, training materials, and plans relating to compliance with the information security program.

- Make available to the FTC every print, broadcast, cable, or Internet advertisement, promotion, form, Web page, email message, or other document that says anything about the collection, use, and security of personal information from or about consumers.

- Make sure all current and future company officers, directors, managers, employees, and contractors who have anything to do with personal consumer information are shown a copy of the agreement.

- Submit a report on compliance with the agreement within six months of the agreement and at any other time the FTC chooses to ask for one.

- Avoid any further misrepresentation of the level of privacy protection that Lilly provides for consumers' personally identifiable information.

This last item is significant because the order lasts twenty years from the date it is issued, or twenty years from the last date that the FTC or other agency files a complaint alleging any violation of the order. In other words, if there is anything like a repeat of the original incident, the company could find itself in several kinds of trouble (which could be the case if Florida's Attorney General acts against the company under that state's Deceptive and Unfair Trade Practices Act in the aforementioned Prozac postal case). Violations of an FTC consent order can result in further sanctions, including civil penalties up to $11,000 per violation.

The cost of fixing the problem and complying with the terms of any settlement you may reach comes on top of any fines that may be involved. For example, fines may be levied to pay for the cost of the investigation. After the FTC settlement, several states sought payment from Eli Lilly for the legal costs they incurred in their own investigations of the incident (paying $160,000 to 8 states). Some observers have suggested that what Eli Lilly agreed to do in response to the Prozac Email Incident was no more than any company should be doing anyway with respect to information protection. However, there is a big—and potentially expensive—difference between carrying out such a program on your own terms and doing it under the watchful eye of others, in this case the FTC *and* privacy watchdogs (the ACLU has already filed requests for copies of all compliance documentation).

Coping Costs

So what would something like the Prozac Email Incident cost your company? Apart from the intangible costs that come from having your brand name tarnished, there are some very tangible costs, starting with the legal bills. If you are facing legal action from either the Federal government or state regulators you will probably want to retain expert external counsel to bolster in-house legal resources. Such experts do not come cheap. You can also bet on there being an overtime bulge in your public relations department.

In March of 2001, Forrester Research issued a landmark analysis of privacy for business titled *Surviving the Privacy Issue*. In this report Forrester quantified the cost of a privacy "blowout." The numbers, shown in Table 2-1, make very interesting reading. The categories into which the costs are broken down are a useful checklist if you want to perform a similar analysis for your company.

Cost of a Privacy Blowout	Small Dot Com		Big Company	
Category	Time (hours)	Cost ($)	Time (hours)	Cost ($)
CEO/president time	86	$ 7,100	48	$ 8,100
Management time	95	$ 5,544	620	$ 38,889
PR Meetings and calls	40	$ 1,067	800	$ 21,333
Management press calls	26	$ 1,778	76	$ 5,456
Management review of privacy practices	15	$ 833	250	$ 13,889
Customer service calls and emails	88	$ 1,944	18,750	$ 416,667
Employee communications and training	1	$ 1,333	18,770	$ 335,889
External consultants		$ 22,500		$ 181,250
Travel		$ 2,000		$ 16,500
		$ 44,099		$ 1,037,973

Table 2-1: Cost of Privacy "Blowout" as estimated by Forrester Research in the 2001 report *Surviving the Privacy Issue*.

As you can see, Forrester performed the same analysis for both a large and a small company. While there is a big difference in the raw numbers, the total costs are probably about the same if you figure them as a percentage of income or revenue or capitalization. In other words, a privacy incident can have a significant impact on the bottom line, whether your company is a small one or a large one.

Note that the costs in Table 2-1 do not include either loss of business or fines imposed by regulators. What they do include is worth a closer look just to be clear on where the impact of the incident will be felt.

- CEO/president time
- Management time
- PR meetings and calls
- Management press calls
- Management review of privacy practices
- Customer service calls and emails
- Employee communications and training
- External consultants
- Travel

Opportunity Costs

Another way to look at the costs of a privacy incident is what it does to the company's stock price. Eli Lilly was trading close to $80 per share right before the incident occurred. Over the next ten days it dropped to $74. However, it soon started to recover and within two months of the incident it was over $80 again. So you could argue that the overall effect of the incident was insignificant, especially when compared with other factors at work that summer, such as the expiration of the patent for Prozac which generated revenues of more than $20 billion in less than a decade, more than a quarter of the company's total revenues. Nevertheless, there is a strong case for saying that any time a company incurs unexpected and avoidable costs it is bad news.

In assessing the impact of this or any other incident there can be no avoiding what economists call "opportunity cost." Simply put, this is what you could have done with the time and money that the incident expended. Suppose that on the first day of the first quarter of the year, a glitch on your Web site reveals the names, phone numbers, and email addresses of several thousand men who have registered for a newsletter about impotence. Some of them are very upset and talk to a lawyer. The press gets hold of the story. You open up your Privacy Incident Response Plan and activate your Privacy Incident Response Team (you will read how to create a PIRP and deploy a PIRT in Chapter 7). Through a combination of Herculean technical, legal, managerial and PR efforts you fix the glitch and diffuse the situation. By the end of the quarter the whole thing is history.

At first, this sounds like success. Suppose that by getting more work out of some people, by shifting some resources around and cutting back on some other expenditures, you accomplished the above with no apparent impact on the bottom line. On several levels this would be considered an amazing accomplishment. Unfortunately, what the law of opportunity cost tells you is that the incident was still bad news for the company. Why? Because if all these efforts had been directed at something else besides recovering from a privacy incident, the bottom line would almost certainly have looked a lot better than it did.

This can be a hard pill to swallow, so to speak, especially if you and your staff are patting yourselves on the back for the great work everyone did to minimize the damage from an incident. But think about the resources the damage control required: public relations, technical, management, legal. With those same resources a new marketing campaign could have been designed, implemented on the web site, and launched in the press. Revenue could have been boosted. That is opportunity cost and that is why it is best to make a concerted effort to avoid such incidents in the first place.

Cost Limits and Gaps

Why would the recommendation be "make a concerted effort to avoid such incidents in the first place" as opposed to "defend against a privacy breach at all costs"? Once again the answer is economics, specifically opportunity costs and diminishing returns, both of which must be factored in when deciding how much to spend to mitigate privacy risks. Such calculations will be familiar to those involved with information security management. Suppose it will cost $1.7 million to install software to protect the confidentiality of your data with powerful 128-bit encryption, but only $1.2 million if you use a weaker option, say 64-bit encryption. Is the $500,000 extra for stronger encryption a worthwhile investment? How likely is it that someone with the resources to break the weaker encryption, but not the stronger encryption, will target your data?

In other words, there comes a point of diminishing returns in any risk reduction plan. In terms of privacy, you probably do need to spend money to beef up your privacy awareness among employees, to perform a privacy audit of your Web site and to participate in a Web privacy seal program. But you can't just keep spending on privacy programs. Their cost must be weighed against other needs within the company.

One way to look at this is "closing-the-gap analysis." This is different from a plain ordinary "gap analysis," which you may have heard mentioned in the context of privacy compliance. Ordinary gap analysis is simply looking at where your organization stands today, relative to some standard with which it needs to comply. This standard may be legislated, as in the case of the Children's Online Privacy Protection Act (COPPA). Or it might be a voluntary standard, such as industry best practices, or an ISO standard. Such gap analysis often precedes and serves as a roadmap for a compliance effort. The purpose of closing-the-gap analysis is to determine at what point your investment in risk reduction measures, ceases to make a meaningful difference.

Consider the chart in Figure 2-2 on the next page. The Y-axis of the chart is the probability of a privacy incident occurring at an organization. The X-axis across the bottom is the number of privacy programs the organization has implemented. Privacy programs is a broadly defined category in this context, encompassing any measures which enhance privacy posture, such as privacy awareness campaigns, privacy training for key employees, privacy audits, and so on.

At first there are no privacy programs and the probability of a privacy incident is high, almost a certainty (where a certainty equals 1.0). Employees are either unaware of the importance of protecting personally identifiable information or not terribly serious about actually protecting it. The effect of the first privacy program is thus considerable, as indicated in the chart. The probability of a privacy incident occurring has been moved closer to zero . The probability is further reduced by the second program, but the effect is less dramatic— the gap between current probability and zero closes by a smaller amount this time, and each time thereafter.

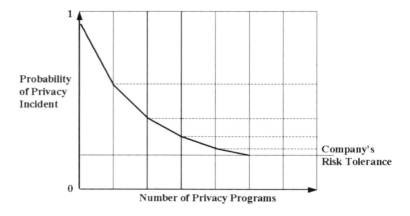

Figure 2-2: Closing-the-gap analysis

How close to zero can, or should, you bring the probability of a privacy incident? That depends upon several factors, including the incremental cost of privacy programs and your company's "risk tolerance." Think of risk tolerance as how comfortable management is with taking a chance that things will go well, given an accurate description of both the risks faced and the mitigation efforts in place to reduce those risks.

As you might expect, different companies, at different stages in different industries, have different risk tolerances. Consider a small startup company creating game software that is licensed to larger companies. The company does not deal directly with the public, has very little contact with personally identifiable information, and is accustomed to living on the edge; risk tolerance is probably high. Take the same company a few years later, when its name has become a household word and its core business has evolved into direct sales of online games that appeal to children, played over the Internet. Risk tolerance is probably a lot lower.

An extensive discussion of risk management theory is clearly beyond the scope of this text. What you need to be thinking about at this point is the balance between your desire to protect the company from damaging privacy incidents and all the other things to which the company needs to pay attention; then allocate resources in order to fulfill its mission. Or to put it another way, it is great that you are concerned about privacy because privacy is very important, but don't lose perspective.

Fines and Other Costs

The cost of a privacy incident can be the fines your company has to pay for breaking certain laws. This was hinted at earlier in relation to Eli Lilly and the Prozac Email Incident, which was investigated under the Federal Trade Commission Act (FTCA). Although Lilly did not pay a federal fine, it did enter into a consent decree, future violations of which can incur fines; and Lilly did pay fines to eight states. The total paid was $160,000 which might sound like a lot if you are a small company, but the Indianapolis-based pharmaceutical giant is not—the fines represented less than $5 per employee, or about half of one percent of what the company CEO earned in 1999.

Numerous companies have paid large fines for violating the Children's Online Privacy Protection Act (COPPA), a law discussed in more detail in Chapter 4. In fact, the FTC marked the first anniversary of the effective date of COPPA by announcing settlements with operators of three Web sites: www.girlslife.com; www.bigmailbox.com; and www.insidetheweb.com. These companies were all charged with illegally collecting personally identifying information from children under 13 years of age without parental consent. They paid a total of $100,000 in civil penalties (they also had to delete all personally identifying information collected from children online at any time since the legislation went into effect).

There is more privacy legislation in the pipeline, with more potential for fines, but Web site privacy problems can have less obvious impacts. One is the lost deal or opportunity. Quite often in business, two or more companies come together for some kind of deal, such as a merger, acquisition, strategic alliance, partnership or capital investment. Normal business practice is for the companies involved to perform due diligence, business-speak for "check them out." Due diligence means asking a lot of questions, such as: Who are these people? How is their credit? What is their reputation? During the last decade a new category of question emerged: How good is their data security? In fact, security consulting companies like the one I used to own were hired to assess information security at companies that were the target of a merger or acquisition.

Now, there is a new category in due diligence, which goes to the heart of Web site privacy practices by asking the question: how "clean" is the PII that a company has collected? The word "clean" can have several meanings in the context of data, for example, there are companies who specialize in cleaning up databases by eliminating duplicate records and correcting some mistakes (such as the wrong state/zip code).

In this context clean means compliant with privacy policies. Suppose that a company which is about to be acquired says, "we have a list of 300,000 people who have given permission for us to send them sales literature." Privacy due diligence requires that assertion be verified. Further suppose that, upon examination of the company's Web site, it appears that all customer email addresses are added to this list, regardless of whether or not they check the box marked:

"Please tell me about new product developments."

The list is thus deemed "dirty," and it will either need to be cleaned up, or its value discounted (lists that are purely opt-in are more valuable than those that are not). Such discrepancies, between list description and list reality, are particularly significant if they are associated with a Web site that has a privacy statement which is specific about how PII will be used, such as a strong statement like "we will NEVER send you offers if you ask us not to." Tempting as it might be, in the heat of a deal, to violate such a pledge, it may not be worth the risk of a privacy incident.

The same temptation arises when a company wants to cash in on data it has collected, not an uncommon business strategy these days. In an article in *Business 2.0* magazine in July, 2001, Warren Packard, managing director for Draper Fisher Jurvetson, a venture capital firm in Redwood City, California, said he was seeing more companies in financial trouble selling off consumer data, and noted:

"It is a concern when someone's business model is not working and they are looking for alternative sources of revenue. The more granular the data you sell, the more you can get for it and some companies are going to get so desperate that they are going to sell their data outside with personally identifiable information."

Note that, in the same article, Packard was asked if he could think of any functioning company that has been punished by the market for conducting a data fire sale. He could not, but that misses the point. If the company that gets into trouble selling its data is already on its way out of business, it is somewhat immune to criticism. However, the buyer of the data needs to be sure they are not paying too much. For example, if a large number of people on the list object to the new owner contacting them, the costs, in terms of complaint calls alone, could cancel out any gain.

Types of Privacy Incident

The following sections discuss the main types of privacy incident. You will be better prepared to develop appropriate responses if you have thought about the different ways in which privacy could become a problem for your company. Bear in mind that the categorization of incidents presented here should not be considered exhaustive. You may think of something specific to your company that does not fall into these categories. If so, be sure to document it for when you get to Chapter 7 and start to prepare your privacy incident response plan.

Security Breach

When a Web site is attacked and security mechanisms fail, the potential clearly exists for a privacy incident. This was the case at the University of Washington Medical Center in March of 2000 when a hacker downloaded medical records, health information and social security numbers of more than 5,000 patients—data which is clearly personally identifiable information or PII. Later that year, Western Union's Web site was hacked and the credit card numbers of 15,700 customers were exposed. More recently, Qwest Communications acknowledged in May of 2002 that its Web-based paperless billing system had stopped checking passwords, allowing anyone who entered a valid username to access that subscriber's billing record, including a complete copy of their most recent phone bill and, if they paid by credit card, the card number and expiration date. Web site security breaches with privacy consequences are typically the result of one or more of the following factors:

■ External Attack: someone with no prior internal knowledge of the company attacks the Web site, or systems containing Web-derived data, thereby compromising PII.

■ Internal Attack: someone inside the company or with inside knowl-edge of the company systems, attacks the Web site or internal systems containing Web-derived data, thereby compromising PII (note that many attacks which appear to be external actually in-volved an internal component).

■ Configuration Error: errors in the configuration of systems that process Web-derived data, or security measures put in place to protect such systems, allow PII to be compromised.

A Security Breach Example

While it is never fun to be the victim of a Web site hack, the conse-quences can vary a great deal according to the type of attack. If the site is simply defaced you can restore it fairly quickly from backups. If PII is compromised, that is, exposed to persons who do not have permission to access it, there is potential for a privacy incident. This was the case in the UWMC and Western Union examples, and a host of other incidents.

At Western Union the incident was particularly embarrassing because the company has built its reputation on safely delivering money, yet here it was, in September of 2000, calling thousands of customers—such as myself—to advise them to cancel the credit cards they had used at the Western Union web site. This was not good news for customers, who had to deal with the hassles of canceling a credit card and the worrying thought that an unethical stranger might have their personal details (see "Consumer Costs" section later in this chapter for more on this topic).

The news was not good for Western Union investors either. Within two days of the story breaking in the press the stock had lost ten percent of its value. Fortunately for Western Union, it is just one part of a large company, First Data, which happens to be the largest processor of credit card transactions in the U.S. The stock price recovered quite quickly as bargain hunters stepped in, but you can wager that being an executive of Western Union during that time was not fun.

A Word to the Wise: If you ever find exposed data, you need to be very careful how you report it. Some people do not take kindly to being told their system is misconfigured, or insecure, or otherwise below par. One way for such persons to mitigate embarrassment and deflect blame is to attack the messenger. A particularly devious strategy on the part of a system owner or manager is to characterize the person reporting the problem as a hacker, a skilled and somehow dubious attacker. Casting matters in this light minimizes the system owner's culpability and may even elicit sympathy; it doesn't do anything good for the messenger.

A few months ago I found, quite by accident, thousands of unprotected personal records on a Web server that was hosting sites for a wide range of professional organizations. No hacking skills were required to get to this data, but I did not want to find myself having to explain this to people less versed in the topic than me (like a judge and/or jury). So I asked a third party to pass along a suggestion to one of the associations: ask your Web hosting company to move PII off the Web server or tighten permissions on the directories in which it is stored. That was enough to prompt the company to improve the security of all of the sites it hosts.

Security or Privacy?

The Western Union incident, like many others over the last ten years, was reported in the media as a security breach. This is technically correct, since what happened was a failure of security. In this case, according to some reports, Western Union had turned off some security mechanisms while they were doing maintenance on the site and a hacker who was probing the site at the time noticed. The hacker gained access and captured the credit card information as proof of this "accomplishment."

According to the three factors listed earlier, this was a combination of External Attack and Configuration Error. The latter is surprisingly common but very few cases are actually made public. When they are, it is often by individuals who could hardly be described as hackers. In the Qwest example it appears that some customers were annoyed that Qwest was not moving quickly enough to fix the problem once it had been reported.

As a Web site operator you need to make sure you have a way of tracking such reports. The problem with data compromise is that, without strong evidence to the contrary, you have to assume it is absolute. In other words, even when it is caused by an honest mistake and is reported by an honest person, you have to assume the worst, unless you can prove that nobody actually saw the data during the time it was visible (something that is very hard to achieve).

According to several accounts, the hacker in the Western Union case was not seeking to profit from the credit card data that was exposed, but that hardly fits the definition of a reliable assumption. The only assumption the company could make was the one it did, the worst one—hence the advice to customers to cancel the cards that had been exposed.

Whilst some people might find the details of such incidents fascinating, most consumers are not interested in the finer points of a security violation. These incidents are, from the consumer perspective, privacy incidents. This is not because consumers cannot think in terms of data security. Many consumers actually implement security concepts such as data classification and access control (in simple terms, for example, there are some things you don't tell certain people). The point is, the data that consumers protect is personal, private data. When that data is exposed, it is perceived as a violation of privacy, not security.

Businesses that operate Web sites should note that the press is increasingly likely to report incidents like the Western Union hack as privacy breaches. The press has picked up on the consumer perspective, partly because the press are also consumers. Most know that if a credit card is compromised they won't have to pay for fraudulent charges, but they will have to go through a lot of effort and aggravation to replace the card. Sadly, there is an increasing probably that they will also know, personally or through a friend or relative, the much greater pain of identity theft (for more on this topic, see the section "Identity Theft" later in this chapter).

Policy Violation

When someone violates your company's Web site privacy policy this can lead to a privacy incident. Suppose there is a form on your Web site where people can request information about your products via email. There is another form where people who need technical support can report a problem and provide an email address for follow up. The Web site privacy notice states that information collected for support purposes will not be used for marketing without permission. If someone emails product marketing information to people who supplied their email addresses for support only, you have a policy violation.

Policy Violation Example

An example of Web site privacy policy violation is the Toysmart case. In July of 2000, Toysmart agreed to settle charges the company violated Section 5 of the FTC Act by misrepresenting to consumers that personal information would *never* be shared with third parties and then disclosing, selling, or offering that information for sale in violation of the company's own privacy statement. The settlement forbid the sale of this customer information except under very limited circumstances. Basically, Toysmart was in financial trouble and sought to sell its mailing lists and customer data. Since the company had promised, in its policy statement, not to do that, the FTC blocked the sale. One lesson here is that companies which seek to acquire PII, as part of a business deal for example, must make sure that the entity selling the data has the right to do so.

As was observed earlier with respect to Eli Lilly, the FTC is apt to see failure to live up to the assurances provided in a privacy policy as a violation of that policy. In other words, you do not have to do anything as flagrant as try to sell PII when you promised you wouldn't for a violation to be called. Consider the Microsoft Passport case, settled by the FTC in the summer of 2002.

Microsoft's privacy policies for Passport, an Internet service that allowed users to sign in at any participating Web site with a single name and password, included statements such as, "Passport achieves a high level of Web Security by using technologies and systems designed to prevent unauthorized access to your personal information" and "Your Passport is protected by powerful online security and a strict privacy policy." According to the FTC's complaint, Microsoft falsely represented that:

> It employs reasonable and appropriate measures under the circumstances to maintain and protect the privacy and confidentiality of consumers' personal information collected through its *Passport* and *Passport Wallet* services, including credit card numbers and billing information stored in Passport Wallet;

> Purchases made with Passport Wallet are generally safer or more secure than purchases made at the same site without Passport Wallet when, in fact, most consumers received identical security at those sites regardless of whether they used Passport Wallet to complete their transactions;

> Passport did not collect any personally identifiable information other than that described in its privacy policy when, in fact, Passport collected and held, for a limited time, a personally identifiable sign-in history for each user; and

> The Kids Passport program provided parents control over what information participating Web sites could collect from their children.

As a result, Microsoft found itself in a similar position to Eli Lilly, having to undertake a series of reforms, all with extensive government oversight. Microsoft has since altered the Passport product substantially and, if you visit Microsoft Web sites today, notably those at its Internet service, MSN, you will see a strong emphasis on privacy. In other words, Microsoft's response to the criticism was to accept it and learn from it, resolving to make privacy a priority rather than a liability.

Privacy Policy Catch-22

As you consider the impact of privacy policy violations, and the more fundamental question of what your privacy policies will be, you do need to be aware of a potential Catch-22: If you post a privacy statement on your Web site to demonstrate your commitment to privacy, you must stick to it, otherwise you could be facing legal problems that would not arise if you did not post such a statement. So making an effort to do the right thing could lead to more trouble than not making an effort. Of course, if you don't post a privacy statement on your Web site you might find people are reluctant to use the site.

What sort of legal trouble are we talking about? In Chapter 4 you will read about a number of laws that are specific to privacy and Web sites. However, several major companies have endured embarrassing Web-related privacy incidents due to a law that is not privacy or Web specific: the Federal Trade Commission Act of 1914. Under section 5(a) of the FTCA: "unfair or deceptive acts or practices in or affecting commerce are declared unlawful." So here is what FTC Chairman Timothy Muris said at the news conference in Washington in August of 2002 announcing the agency's settlement with Microsoft over the Passport charges:

> "Companies that promise to keep personal information secure must follow reasonable and appropriate measures to do so. It is not only good business, it's the law. Even absent known security breaches, we will not wait to act."

Taken together with the FTC's action in the Prozac Email Incident described earlier, this is a clear signal that privacy statements must be adhered to, by law. This is a topic that will be revisited in Chapter 6. For now, ponder the words of Computerworld's Patrick Thibodeau:

> "In its enforcement action against Microsoft Corp. this week, the U.S. Federal Trade Commission demonstrated its ability, once again, to hang companies with their own words."

Policy Change

If there is one thing that companies can learn from the wild business cycles of the last few years it is that things change, sometimes very rapidly. Markets shift, business models change, technology advances. Not surprisingly, it can be hard for the company Web site to keep pace. Most companies recognize this when they craft a privacy statement for their Web site, typically including language that will allow for future changes to privacy policy. Here are two examples:

> "Sears.com may update this policy from time to time. Please check our policy periodically for changes."

"The Lycos Network will update this policy from time to time so please check back periodically. When such changes occur, you will see the word "Updated" next to the Privacy Policy link on the front page of each site on the Lycos Network. If at any point we decide to use personally identifiable information in a manner different from that stated at the time it was collected, we will prominently post such changes prior to implementing them."

Unfortunately, some companies have failed to warn people that the privacy policy may change. Others have made changes that exceed what some people consider acceptable. In other words, even if you tell people the policy may change, you cannot expect to escape criticism if you make a major change in the direction of less privacy protection.

Policy Change Example

To find out what sort of problems companies have encountered with privacy policy changes, simply go to google.com and use the following search phrase: privacy policy change uproar. At the top of the search results you will probably find a story about Yahoo. In March of 2002, this major Web portal changed the "marketing preferences" page by which users give, or decline, permission for Yahoo to send them promotional email. In so doing, the company reset the default preferences for all members, requiring them to manually request blocking of future messages, even if, in the past, they had declined to accept such email.

This action was roundly criticized by many Yahoo users and privacy advocates added their voices to the clamor. Whether Yahoo actually suffered any loss of business directly attributable to this incident is hard to tell. The effect was more likely a tarnishing of the brand. A lot of people who experienced this incident lost a measure of respect for the company, which may affect their future choices about Web services.

Note that Yahoo had planned to notify everyone who would be affected by the change, but word of the change got out before everyone was notified. This only compounded the criticism since a lot of users found out about the change in the press, before they were told by Yahoo. Also note that Yahoo is by no means the only big name Web site to be criticized for a change in policy.

Policy Criticism

Public criticism of your company's Web site privacy policy can come from several quarters. Such criticism can be triggered by a change, as discussed in the previous section, but it can also be triggered simply by someone deciding that the policy, as it is, has problems.

Policy Criticism Example

For an example of a company facing criticism of its privacy policy you need look no further than the Web's largest auction site, eBay.com. In March of 2002, eBay faced a huge wave of criticism and a call for the FTC to investigate changes to eBay's privacy policy for possible "unfair or deceptive trade practices." While this wave of criticism was triggered by a change in policy, the very vocal objections to the change caused more people to read the company's privacy statement and find fault with things that had been there for some time. Here is how Jason Catlett, President of junkbusters.com, described eBay's privacy policy:

> "a repulsive confection of excessively broad disclaimers of liability coated in marketing sugar that deceitfully attempts to disguise the awfulness of its position."

Criticism and Correction

As in other areas of business, there are several ways that a smart company can use an outbreak of criticism over privacy to make friends and influence people. One option is to accept the criticism. That is what eBay did in March of 2002 when it backed off the change that had generated so much negative reaction. Although this response was not enough to satisfy many privacy advocates, one suspects that the average eBay user was favorably impressed: the company certainly appeared to be sensitive to privacy concerns. There will be more about handling such situations in Chapter 7.

Of course, avoiding criticism in the first place is usually the least costly option. Consider the case of DoubleClick, one of the largest Internet advertising companies. In June of 1999, the company announced that it would acquire Abacus, a company that had accumulated large amounts of non-Internet information about people, referred to as off-line data (in this case, some 80 million households, profiled from direct mail catalogue purchases). Privacy advocates immediately expressed concern about the possible combining of the Abacus data with the online data that DoubleClick had been accumulating by tracking Web surfers through online advertisements. Concern had already been expressed over DoubleClick's "secret" tracking of Web users through cookies.

As a result of what can be construed as a failure to anticipate privacy policy criticism, DoublecCick has faced class action lawsuits, FTC investigations, and action by the Attorneys General from ten states. In August of 2002, DoubleClick agreed to pay $450,000 to settle with those states, and dramatically alter the way it operates, beginning with major changes to its privacy policies and notices (the settlement document in this case actually provides an excellent description of how DoubleClick's complex cookie system worked, as well as the numerous measures with which the company now has to comply—see www.oag.state.ny.us for details).

Sensitive Data: Each new privacy case seems to expand the privacy language. The DoubleClick settlement with the states defines a "sensitive data" category that will probably play a role in future privacy cases. Sensitive data "includes but is not limited to data related to an individual's health or medical condition, sexual behavior or orientation, or detailed personal finances, information that appears to relate to children under 13, racial or ethnic origin, political opinions, religious or philosophical opinions or beliefs and trade union membership; PII obtained from individuals who were children under the age of 13 at the time of data collection; and PII otherwise protected under federal law (for example, cable subscriber information or video rental records)."

Like Eli Lilly, DoubleClick will have to live with the compliance guidelines for a number of years. In addition, the company must now provide privacy education, not only to own its employees, but also to the companies who use its services (these include some of the biggest names on the Web, including washingtonpost.com and CNN.com). Furthermore, as a result of the $1.8 million class action settlement, DoubleClick must conduct a public information campaign consisting of 300 million banner ads that educate consumers on Internet privacy. Moreover, the company must retain an independent accounting firm to conduct an annual review regarding compliance with the settlement. (Note that this settlement was not tough enough for some privacy advocates, who are still seeking to have it overturned).

Consumer Costs

Clearly, companies can pay quite a price for a privacy breach, but what price does the consumer pay? Several cases of compromised credit cards have been mention in this chapter and it was pointed out that most consumers are not liable for fraudulent charges on compromised credit cards. However, it may be a mistake to look at the cost of a privacy breach to the consumer strictly in terms of money.

Aggravation

Companies should not underestimate the consumer aggravation factor of something like a credit card being compromised. For a start, these days an individual may have five or six monthly bills automatically paid by credit card. If the card has to be cancelled, all of those companies need to be contacted and provided with an alternative card or means of payment. If that is not done in time, bills can bounce and services can be interrupted. Perhaps even trickier are the annual subscriptions a person has placed on their cancelled credit card. These are easy to overlook when you sit down to deal with a compromised card. You don't have to loose any money in fraudulent charges for a cancelled card to cost you a lot of wasted time on hold, trying to mitigate the damage.

Identity Theft

A growing fear among consumers is that any of their personal data which is compromised will be the starting point for a identity thief. As was noted in Chapter 1, identity theft is a very real concern for consumers because it can create very real suffering, as well as create serious problems that require a lot of time and money to correct. To understand the connection between your Web site and the crime of identity theft you first need to understand what an identity thief does. Here is a description used by the Federal Trade Commission, the agency charged with taking the lead on this issue:

> "An identity thief co-opts some piece of your personal information and appropriates it without your knowledge to commit fraud or theft. An all-too-common example is when an identity thief uses your personal information to open a credit card account in your name."

The problem is certainly on the increase. In 1999, the FTC created something called the Identity Theft Data Clearinghouse to try and get a clearer picture of the nature and prevalence of identity theft. In 2000, the first full year of operation, the agency entered more than 31,000 consumer complaints into the database. In 2001, that number grew to 86,168. As of the end of May, 2002, only five months into the calendar year, 55,000 complaints have already been added to the database. Here are some of the ways imposters can get personal information and take over someone's identity.

How identity thieves get your personal information:

■ They steal wallets and purses containing your identification and credit and bank cards.

■ They steal your mail, including your bank and credit card statements, pre-approved credit offers, telephone calling cards and tax information.

■ They complete a "change of address form" to divert your mail to another location.

■ They rummage through your trash, or the trash of businesses, for personal data in a practice known as "dumpster diving."

■ They fraudulently obtain your credit report by posing as a landlord, employer or someone else who may have a legitimate need for — and a legal right to — the information.

■ They get your business or personnel records at work.

■ They find personal information in your home.

■ They use personal information you share on the Internet.

■ They buy your personal information from "inside" sources. For example, an identity thief may pay a store employee for information about you that appears on an application for goods, services or credit.

How identity thieves use your personal information:

■ They call your credit card issuer and, pretending to be you, ask to change the mailing address on your credit card account. The imposter then runs up charges on your account. Because your bills are being sent to the new address, it may take some time before you realize there's a problem.

■ They open a new credit card account, using your name, date of birth and SSN. When they use the credit card and don't pay the bills, the delinquent account is reported on your credit report.

■ They establish phone or wireless service in your name.

■ They open a bank account in your name and write bad checks on that account.

■ They file for bankruptcy under your name to avoid paying debts they've incurred under your name, or to avoid eviction.

■ They counterfeit checks or debit cards, and drain your bank account.

■ They buy cars by taking out auto loans in your name.

Loss of Privacy

Finally, it has to be said that many consumers see the main cost of a privacy breach as something very intangible and hard to define, yet very real: loss of personal privacy. Putting a price on personal privacy is not easy. I suspect that we have not yet seen anything like the upper limit on what a jury might award in a privacy case. What we have seen is a significant shift in perception. Consider the case of Ziff Davis Media, which settled a case with Attorneys General from several states in the summer of 2002, over what was originally reported, when it happened in 2001, as a security breach, but was later characterized as a privacy incident.

The New York Attorney General's office got involved after it was discovered that about 12,000 subscription orders were easily accessible on a Web site that the company used to accept orders for its magazines. For several days after a coding error was made, apparently during the execution of an internal marketing project, anyone on the Web who knew where to look was able to download a 1.3 megabyte text file of names, mailing addresses, email addresses and, in about fifty cases, credit card numbers. In the settlement, the company agreed to pay $500 to each of the approximately fifty U.S. consumers whose credit card data were exposed, regardless of whether they incurred fraudulent charges. The company also agree to implement new online privacy controls and pay the New York Department of Law $100,000 to be split among the states involved. New York's Attorney, General Eliot Spitzer, said the following in the settlement announcement:

> "The company's privacy policy promised reasonable security, but it was not effective in this case. With identity theft on the rise, consumers expect online businesses to recognize the sensitivity of personal contact and credit card information and to take reasonable measures to protect that information."

While the fines in this case might not sound like a lot of money, they establish a basis for further claims. When a company stipulates the facts in a settlement like this, even one in which they do not admit to breaking any laws, the groundwork is laid for other parties, such as someone whose identity was stolen as a result of the incident, to go to court.

CHAPTER THREE

WEB PRIVACY PRINCIPLES

"The right to be left alone—the most comprehensive of rights, and the right most valued by a free people."

—Justice Louis Brandeis, Olmstead v. United States, 1928.

3: WEB PRIVACY PRINCIPLES

The way people feel about sharing personal information—especially computerized information—can vary significantly, between countries, between companies, and between individuals. However, some general principles have evolved over the years and have been widely accepted in many quarters. The goal of this chapter is to review these principles and understand their importance to businessesthat have Web operation and use email for customer contact.

Basic Privacy Principles

Why do you need to be aware of basic privacy principles? The main reason is that a lot of privacy law in the United States today is based upon them. You can see these basic privacy principles at work in laws which impose specific legal requirements on Web sites, such as the Children's Online Privacy Protection Act (COPPA: 1998) and the Health Insurance Portability and Accountability Act (HIPAA: 1996). These laws are described in more detail in Chapter 4. Basic privacy principles have also shaped older laws such as the Fair Credit Reporting Act (FCRA: 1970), as well as legal actions and regulatory decisions regarding privacy, such as those by the FTC against Eli Lilly, Doubleclick, and Microsoft.

The second reason for knowing about these principles is that they have guided the privacy legislation of many countries outside the U.S. In fact, some countries have elevated basic privacy principles to the level of privacy *rights*, which means that in many cases, personal data enjoys legal protection by default. This is not the case in the U.S., which has taken a piecemeal approach to privacy legislation. For example, there are more than 30 federal laws that address data privacy topics as specific as video rental records, school records, and the use of driver's license data. Thus, some personal data are protected by federal laws, others are not. At the same time a complex patchwork of privacy laws exists at the state level—also drawing on basic privacy principles—and there is a growing body of privacy case law arising from legal actions brought by individuals and regulators.

More privacy laws will probably be enacted at the federal level in the next few years, and they will tend to mirror basic privacy principles. Certainly more American companies are engaging in international business via the Web. So another reason for acquainting oneself with these privacy principles is their ability to provide a default approach to privacy that will meet standards for best practices well into the future, and just about anywhere your business takes you. A good example of this is Apple Computer, which has committed itself to a "highest common denominator" approach to privacy, intending to meet international privacy standards even when they are higher than domestic requirements.

Early U.S. Laws

The first major federal legislation to reflect basic privacy principles was perhaps the Freedom of Information Act, or FOIA, enacted in 1966. The FOIA established the general principle that any person has a right of access to federal agency records. The FOIA provides access to all federal records (or portions of those records) except those protected from release by nine specific exemptions:

1. classified national defense and foreign relations information,

2. internal agency personnel rules and practices,

3. material prohibited from disclosure by another law,

4. trade secrets and other confidential business information,

5. certain inter-agency or intra-agency communications,

6. personnel, medical, and other files involving personal privacy,

7. certain records compiled for law enforcement purposes,

8. matters relating to the supervision of financial institutions, and

9. geological information on oil wells.

The FOIA does not apply to Congress or the courts, nor does it apply to records of state or local governments. However, nearly all state governments have their own FOIA-type statutes. The FOIA does not require a private organization or business to release any information directly to the public, whether it has been submitted to the government or not. However, information submitted by private firms to the federal government may be available through a FOIA request provided that the information is not a trade secret, confidential business information, or protected by some other exemption.

Closely related to the Freedom of Information Act is the Privacy Act, another federal law regarding federal government records. The Privacy Act, the emergence of which will be discussed in a moment, establishes certain controls over how the executive branch agencies of the federal government gather, maintain, and disseminate personal information (like the FOIA, the Privacy Act can also be used to obtain access to information, but it pertains only to records the federal government keeps on individual citizens and lawfully admitted resident aliens; the FOIA covers all records under the custody and control of federal executive branch agencies).

The Fair Credit Reporting Act of 1970 was probably the first federal legislation in the United States to refer to "the consumer's right to privacy." However, this law it very narrowly focused and does not specifically address computer-based information. The FCRA, which was substantially overhauled in 1996 by the Consumer Credit Reporting Reform Act (CCRRA) had a very narrow intent: to protect consumers from the disclosure of inaccurate and arbitrary personal information held by consumer reporting agencies. Although the FCRA regulated the disclosure of personal information, it did not restrict the amount or type of information that could be collected.

The Hew Report

You might be surprised to learn that the first U.S. legislation to consider privacy specifically in the context of computers appeared in the early seventies. Elliot Richardson, who was Richard Nixon's Secretary for Health, Education and Welfare, commissioned a study of record-keeping practices in the computer age. The resulting report, commonly known as the "HEW Report," recommended the enactment of a federal "Code of Fair Information Practice" for all automated personal data systems. The code envisioned by HEW contained five principles that would be given legal effect as "safeguard requirements" for automated personal data systems:

1. There must be no personal data record keeping systems whose existence is secret.

2. There must be a way for an individual to find out what information about him is in a record and how it is used.

3. There must be a way for an individual to prevent information about him that was obtained for one purpose being used or made available for other purposes without his consent.

4. There must be a way for an individual to correct or amend a record of identifiable information about him.

5. Any organization creating, maintaining, using, or disseminating records of identifiable personal data must assure the reliability of the data for their intended use and must take precautions to prevent misuse of the data.

While it is unlikely to impact business Web sites directly, the Privacy Act of 1974 is worth knowing about because it embodied the HEW principles in law, establishing protections for personal data held by the federal government. And although the law only applies to the federal government, it is important to note that the federal government compiles a wide range of information on individuals. For example, if you were ever in the military or employed by a federal agency, there should be records of your service. If you have ever applied for a federal grant or received a student loan guaranteed by the government, you are probably the subject of a file. There are records on every individual who has ever paid income taxes or received a check from Social Security or Medicare.

The Privacy Act establishes certain controls over what personal information is collected by the federal government and how it is used. The Act guarantees three primary rights:

1. the right to see records about yourself, subject to the Privacy Act's exemptions,

2. the right to amend that record if it is inaccurate, irrelevant, untimely, or incomplete, and

3. the right to sue the government for violations of the statute including permitting others to see your records unless specifically permitted by the Act.

The Privacy Act also provides for certain limitations on agency information practices, such as requiring that information about a person be collected directly from that person to the greatest extent practicable; requiring agencies to ensure that their records are relevant, accurate, timely, and complete. ; It also prohibits agencies from maintaining information describing how an individual exercises his or her First Amendment rights unless the individual consents to it, a statute permits it, or it is within the scope of an authorized law enforcement investigation (note that this description of the Privacy Act, and some of the preceding documentation of the FOIA, are taken from public domain documents published by the federal government).

The OECD Guidelines

Another important set of data privacy principles was published in 1980 by the Organization for Economic Cooperation and Development. The OECD is comprised of thirty countries bound together by three principles: pluralistic democracy, respect for human rights, and open market economies. The OECD's "Guidelines on the Protection of Privacy and Transborder Flows of Personal Data" were adopted by the organization in 1980 in support of these principles. The full text of the document, which is often referred to simply as "the OECD Guidelines," can be read online at the OECD web site (www.oecd.org). You can also buy a hard copy or license a printable electronic version. The following is a summary of the privacy principles the document sets forth:

- **Collection Limitation Principle**: There should be limits to the collection of personal data and any such data should be obtained by lawful and fair means and, where appropriate, with the knowledge or consent of the data subject.

- **Data Quality Principle**: Personal data should be relevant to the purposes for which they are to be used, and, to the extent necessary for those purposes, should be accurate, complete and kept up-to-date.

- **Purpose Specification Principle**: The purposes for which personal data are collected should be specified not later than at the time of data collection and the subsequent use limited to the fulfillment of those purposes or such others as are not incompatible with those purposes and as are specified on each occasion of change of purpose.

- **Use Limitation Principle**: Personal data should not be disclosed, made available or otherwise used for purposes other than those specified in the Purpose Specification Principle, except with the consent of the data subject or by the authority of law.

- **Security Safeguards Principle**: Personal data should be protected by reasonable security safeguards against such risks as loss or unauthorized access, destruction, use, modification or disclosure of data.

- **Openness Principle**: There should be a general policy of openness about developments, practices and policies with respect to personal data. Means should be readily available of establishing the existence and nature of personal data, and the main purposes of their use, as well as the identity and usual residence of the Data Controller.

- **Individual Participation Principle**: An individual should have the right:

a) to obtain from a data controller, or otherwise, confirmation of whether or not the data controller has data relating to him;

b) to have communicated to him, data relating to him within a reasonable time; at a charge, if any, that is not excessive; in a reasonable manner; and in a form that is readily intelligible to him;

c) to be given reasons if a request made under subparagraphs (a) and (b) is denied, and to be able to challenge such denial; and

d) to challenge data relating to him and, if the challenge is successful to have the data erased, rectified, completed or amended.

- **Accountability Principle**: A Data Controller should be accountable for complying with measures that give effect to the principles stated above.

These principles have guided the development of privacy laws in many countries, including Canada, Australia, Singapore, Hong Kong, and the fifteen member countries of the European Union (E.U.). For example, you can see them reflected in the U.K. Data Protection Act of 1998, which includes a statement of eight enforceable principles of good practice with which anyone processing personal data must comply. These state that data must be:

• fairly and lawfully processed;

• processed for limited purposes;

• adequate, relevant and not excessive;

• accurate;

• not kept longer than necessary;

• processed in accordance with the data subject's rights;

• secure;

• not transferred to countries without adequate protection.

1984! The first U.K. Data Protection Act was passed in 1984. By the time it was revised in 1998, personal data was being defined very broadly, to include "both facts and opinions about the individual" and "information regarding the intentions of the data controller towards the individual." The definition of processing was also widened and now incorporates the concepts of 'obtaining', 'holding' and 'disclosing.'

As you can see there are many similarities between the OECD and U.K. principles and those in the HEW Report. However, you may have noticed several terms that are not in the HEW principles: data subject, data controller, and transborder data flows. Each of these will be explained in turn, starting with data subject, which, as we noted in Chapter 1, is simply a handy way of saying "the individual described or identified by the data."

Data Controller

The term data controller is more complex and refers to a concept that is widely used in Europe but less so in the United States. Here is how data controller is defined in Britain's Data Protection Act:

"a person who (either alone or jointly or in common with other persons) determines the purposes for which and the manner in which any personal data are, or are to be, processed."

In Europe the concept of a data controller is seen as essential to the implementation of basic privacy principles such as those in the HEW Report, namely:

• finding out what information about yourself is in a record,

• preventing information about yourself that was obtained for one purpose from being used or made available for other purposes without your consent,

• correcting or amending a record of identifiable information about yourself.

In other words, unless there is a way to identify persons in control of personal data, it is very hard to protect the privacy of the persons described by the data, the data subjects. Thus the accountability principle specifically refers to the role of the data controller. The British law stresses the importance of establishing whether or not someone is a data controller, because it is data controllers who are required to comply with the data protection principles. Section 4 of the Act states:

"it shall be the duty of a data controller to comply with the data protection principles in relation to all personal data with respect to which he is the data controller."

Under privacy protection laws in Britain, and many other European countries, a data controller is a "person" in the legal sense, a term which comprises not only individuals but also organizations such as companies and other corporate and unincorporated bodies of persons (for example, a homeowners' association, a country club, a public company, or a sole proprietor). If your company does business in Europe it is almost certain to be a data controller.

Transborder Data Flows

One of the main motives for the OECD to develop privacy guidelines was the need to encourage international harmonization of privacy laws, without which the free flow of economically necessary personal information could be interrupted. In other words, more than two decades ago the OECD anticipated that cultural and political differences between Members—the countries that make up the OECD refer to themselves as Members—could result in differing standards for data protection, which might create a reluctance to allow personal data to cross borders, thereby impeding business.

No Flow: There are several examples of differing standards for data protection resulting in reluctance to allow personal data to cross borders. In 1991 an airline operating under Swedish law was not allowed to deliver personal data to U.S. Customs without first warning passengers of the inadequacies of U.S. data-protection laws, and therefore obtaining informed consent. In another case, a German data processing bureau was prevented from carrying out its processing in the United Kingdom, due to inadequacies in U.K. law. France even required contractual guarantees of adherence to French law before Mormon genealogical records could be transferred to Utah.

As the OECD Guidelines state: "although national laws and policies may differ, Member countries have a common interest in protecting privacy and individual liberties, and in reconciling fundamental but competing values such as privacy and the free flow of information." The Guidelines also note "automatic processing and transborder flows of personal data create new forms of relationships among countries and require the development of compatible rules and practices." Since the flow of personal data across borders contributes to economic and social development it would be undesirable for "domestic legislation concerning privacy protection and transborder flows of personal data" to hinder such flows. The Guidelines thus recommend that Member countries:

1. take into account in their domestic legislation the principles concerning the protection of privacy and individual liberties (that is, the ones summarized above);

2. endeavor to remove or avoid creating, in the name of privacy protection, unjustified obstacles to transborder flows of personal data;

3. co-operate in the implementation of the Guidelines;

4. agree as soon as possible on specific procedures of consultation

and co-operation for the application of these Guidelines.

In 1985 the OECD followed through on item four by publishing the "Declaration on Transborder Data Flows." This was further evidence of the desire of Member countries to affirm the general spirit in which they would address these issues. The Declaration began by acknowledging that computerized data and information were now circulating freely on an international scale and significant progress had been achieved in the area of privacy protection at national and international levels. It then stated the four things Member countries would do to further their goals:

1. *Promote* access to data and information and related services, and avoid the creation of unjustified barriers to the international exchange of data and information;

2. *Seek* transparency in regulations and policies relating to information, computer and communications services affecting transborder data flows;

3. *Develop* common approaches for dealing with issues related to transborder data flows and, when appropriate, develop harmonized solutions;

4. *Consider* possible implications for other countries when dealing with issues related to transborder data flows.

This might sound like very abstract, high-level stuff, but it does have practical implications for Web site privacy, especially if you operate multiple Web sites in different countries, or even one site in one country that processes personal data from multiple countries. Chapter 5 will address the practical implications of transborder personal data flows, including several means by which companies can avoid some of the problems that can arise when such data needs to flow into the United States. The point to note here is that the privacy principles at work internationally were established some time ago and at a very high level.

Fair Information Practice Principles

So, basic data privacy principles were being discussed long before the commercialization of the Internet. In 1998, the U.S. Federal Trade Commission reiterated these principles in the context of the

Internet when it produced, at the request of the legislative branch, a document called "Privacy Online: A Report to Congress." The report began by observing that:

> "Over the past quarter century, government agencies in the United States, Canada, and Europe have studied the manner in which entities collect and use personal information — their "information practices" — and the safeguards required to assure those practices are fair and provide adequate privacy protection. The result has been a series of reports, guidelines, and model codes that represent widely-accepted principles concerning fair information practices."

Since its publication, this report has helped to shape the current "privacy-enforcement" role of the FTC. This role, about which every Web site operator needs to know, is discussed in Chapters 2 and 6. In this chapter, we focus on the five core principles of privacy protection that the FTC determined were "widely-accepted," namely: Notice/Awareness, Choice/Consent, Access/Participation, Integrity/Security, and Enforcement/Redress. Each will be described in turn, together with some practical implications.

Notice/Awareness

Notice is a concept that should be familiar to network professionals. Many systems, including many Web sites, put users on notice with respect to ownership, security, and terms of use. Such notice might be a banner that appears during network log-on, warning that access to the network is restricted to authorized users. It might be a splash page for a Web site informing visitors that clicking to enter constitutes agreement to the terms of use. In the context of Web site privacy, notice means you must advise visitors to your site of your policies with respect to the personal data you process. As the FTC puts it:

> "Consumers should be given notice of an entity's information practices before any personal information is collected from them. Without notice, a consumer cannot make an informed decision as to whether and to what extent to disclose personal information. Moreover, three of the other principles (choice/consent, access/participation, and enforcement/redress) are only meaningful when a consumer

has notice of an entity's policies, and his or her rights with respect thereto."

In practical terms, the primary means of providing privacy notice to Web site visitors is the privacy statement, described in Chapter 1 and discussed in detail in Chapter 6. For simple sites that set no cookies or receive no user input, such a statement is easy to draft. The more complex and interactive the site, the more work it will take to craft a statement that covers all the bases. Here are the main points that need to be covered:

- Identification of the entity collecting the data.

- Identification of the intended use of the data.

- Identification of any potential recipients of the data.

- The nature of the data collected and the means by which it is collected, if not obvious (for example, passively, by means of electronic monitoring, or actively, by asking the consumer to provide the information).

- Whether the provision of the requested data is voluntary or required, and the consequences of a refusal to provide the requested information.

- The steps taken by the data collector to ensure the confidentiality, integrity, and quality of the data.

Of course, it might not be your job to pull together this information and come up with a privacy statement—in recent years, many large organizations have been appointing chief privacy officers to oversee the creation of privacy policies for the organization and its Web sites. Nevertheless, if you are responsible for the Web site, you may be asked to do some of the work, notably documenting logging activity and the use of cookies. The following sections briefly discuss these issues and they are addressed again—in the context of writing privacy statements—in Chapter 6.

Logging Activity: You need to let visitors to your site know if you use automated tools to log information about their visits (information such as the type of browser and operating system they used to access your site, the date and time they accessed the site, the pages they viewed, and the paths that they took through the site).

Use of Web Bugs and Beacons: Use of these techniques should be disclosed, along with a clear statement of how and why they are used, and what information they track. (for more on this topic, see Chapter 6 and the Sources section at the end of the book).

Use of Cookies: Use of cookies should be disclosed and a distinction should be made between *session* cookies, which expire when the user closes the Web browser, and *persistent* cookies, which are downloaded to the user's machine for future use on the site.

Choice/Consent

Like Notice/Awareness, this second principle should be addressed with honesty and sensitivity. *Choice* means giving consumers options as to how any personal information collected from them may be used. This relates to secondary uses of information, which the FTC describes as "uses beyond those necessary to complete the contemplated transaction." The FTC notes that "such secondary uses can be internal, such as placing the consumer on the collecting company's mailing list in order to market additional products or promotions, or external, such as the transfer of information to third parties."

Whether or not you are involved in deciding what use is made of personal information that comes from your Web site, you need to know whether you are going to give users of the site any choice in the matter, even if it is something as simple as a check box that says "You may e-mail me about special offers on related products." As you might expect, privacy advocates prefer the opt-in form of consent, in which people specifically request to be included on a mailing list, rather than opt-out, which adds people to the list by default, until such time as they request to be removed (there is more on these terms in the section "Options for Opting, " later in the chapter).

Access/Participation

The point of *access* and *participation* is to let people about whom you have information find out what that information is, and contest its accuracy and completeness if they believe it is wrong. Many online systems currently lack the means to implement such processes securely. However, access is considered an essential element of fair information practices and privacy protection. In the context of business Web sites, the main obstacle to providing access and participation is a lack of cheap and secure methods of reliably identifying, that is, authenticating, the data subjects.

Compliance with U.S. laws that mandate access, such as the Fair Credit Reporting Act, is accomplished right now through more traditional channels of communication, such as letters and faxes. Both require human participation and review. Unless you have a high level of assurance that you are giving online access to the appropriate person—such as multiple factor authentication—there is a serious risk that providing access in support of privacy will actually lead to privacy breaches (for example, through unauthorized disclosure to someone posing as the data subject).

Watch Out: More and more companies are finding that the cost of communicating with customers via the Web and e-mail is much lower than communicating via voice or paper. Consequently, management will want to explore, sooner or later, data subject access to company PII databases through the Web site and/or e-mail. Unfortunately, until the security of the underlying technology improves, this strategy is fraught with risks, such as unauthorized disclosure through spoofing, pretexting, or the interception of unencrypted e-mail. Do not attempt unless management is fully aware of the risks and prepared to fund appropriate levels of additional security.

Integrity/Security

The fourth widely accepted principle is that data be *accurate* and *secure*. To assure data *integrity*, data collectors, like Web sites, must take reasonable steps, such as using only reputable sources of data and cross-referencing data against multiple sources, providing consumer access to data, and destroying untimely data or converting it to anonymous form. Security involves both managerial and technical measures to protect against loss and the unauthorized access, destruction, use, or disclosure of the data. Managerial measures include internal organizational measures that limit access to data and ensure that those individuals with access do not utilize the data for unauthorized purposes. Technical security measures to prevent unauthorized access include the following:

- Limiting access through access control lists (ACLs), network passwords, database security, and other methods

- Storing data on secure servers that cannot be accessed via the Internet or modem

- Encryption of data during transmission and storage (Secure Sockets Layer, or SSL, is considered acceptable when submitting information via a Web site—but note that, unless the client system has a digital certificate or other authentication upon which the server can rely, SSL may not be acceptable for disclosure from server to client).

Enforcement/Redress

The FTC has observed that "the core principles of privacy protection can only be effective if there is a mechanism in place to enforce them." What that mechanism is for your Web site will depend on several factors. As you will see in the next chapter, your Web site may have to comply with specific privacy laws. Your organization may subscribe to an industry code of practice or *privacy seal program*, both of which may include dispute resolution mechanisms and consequences for failure to comply with program requirements. A private action against your organization is also a possibility if the organization is found to be responsible for a breach of privacy that caused harm to an individual. Class-action lawsuits have also been brought, alleging privacy invasion. In Chapter 2, the general oversight role of the government was discussed; specifically the willingness of the FTC to find that failure to live up to privacy policies constitutes deceptive business practice.

Options for Opting

Before concluding this chapter and our review of privacy principles, some practical consideration must be given to the principle of choice and the terms "opt-in" and "opt-out." Visitors to a commercial Web site typically make a number of choices about the use and disclosure of their personal information. For example, the site may allow visitors to make purchases. Visitors supply their name and other information necessary to complete a purchase transaction, typically via a user input form. Reference has already been made to the value of reinforcing general privacy notices with specific notices on forms. For example, a product order form might state that information submitted via the form will be used to complete the order and nothing more.

Of course, if a visitor to your Web site has gone so far as to start filling out an order form, you may want to make the most of the opportunity. For example, in the offline world it is standard practice to mail catalogues and product news to people who have purchased from you. Some people appreciate this, others object, usually by requesting that you stop sending mail to them. In other words, the customer has a choice to *opt-out* of your mailing list.

Things work a little differently online, mainly because people perceive email to be quite different from postal mail (see "Email Costs"). So, to continue our example of Web site visitors who are interested in purchasing your products or services, you may want to think twice before assuming that this interest equates to permission to send them email that is not directly related to that purchase. What you can do, entirely in keeping with basic privacy principles, is give people a choice. You can include on the purchase form a suitable check box, labeled "Keep me informed of new products," or whatever choice it is you wish to offer, whatever permission you would like to have.

Email Costs! Whereas postal mail is paid for entirely by the sender, email is paid for, at least in part, by the people who receive it (through fees to the recipient's Internet Service Provider). Also, weeding out unwanted email is considered by many people to be more of a chore than ditching unwanted postal mail. Most Americans get one postal delivery per day per household. Compare that to the number of times per day the average email user gets a fresh batch of email delivered to his or her in-basket. Sorting out the unwanted email is not a once-a-day chore you can delegate, but a constant, personal distraction; hence the sensitivity that many people have developed to getting email they don't want.

The next consideration is whether or not the box is checked by default. Presenting the form with an unchecked box requires persons using the form to positively affirm their decision; in other words they *opt-in*. From a privacy perspective, this is the preferred approach to building mailing lists, particularly emailing lists.

Pre-checking a permission check box is generally frowned upon as presumptuous. Privacy advocates would argue that is the same as opt-out, that is, the person's permission is assumed, and their choice made for them rather than by them.

Some privacy advocates would like to go further and require what is known as *confirmed opt-in* or *double opt-in*. In this example, conformed opt-in means that when someone checks the box and gives permission to be contacted, the company then confirms this— for example, send the person an e-mail saying "You indicated that we may e-mail you about special offers on related products—please confirm this by replying to this message."

While confirmed opt-in might seem like overkill, and may result in fewer names being added to your list—if there is no confirming email, the address cannot be added—there are some practical benefits. If you have ever worked with an opt-in list that did not require confirmation, you will know that a surprising number of people make mistakes when typing their e-mail addresses (which is why some forms require you to enter your email address twice). If someone who wants information from you enters her email address incorrectly, you both loose. She doesn't get the information she presumably wanted and, unless you have some other means of contact such as telephone or postal mail, you have no way of asking her to correct her email address. The confirmed opt-in method assures you that you are using a valid e-mail address for that person and you have their choice well and truly documented.

Addressing Email : There are several ways of improving your chances of getting a good email address when you ask for one. You can use a duplicate email address field and make sure the user types the same address twice. Unfortunately, some people simply do not know their email address (some think it is the alias that appears in an Outlook header, such as "Cobb, Stephen"). So you may want to validate the user input to make sure it fits these parameters: at least one allowable character preceding the @ character, followed by at least one allowable character and a dot, ending in a legal domain name (the definition of legal domain name in programming logic is a complex task, since there can be subdomains, but working back from the end on an address is one way to determine where an address is from, geographically speaking, which can be useful).

Marketers have tended to favor the *opt-out* approach to choice, which has several levels, the most basic being to use a person's information without any permission, until such time as he or she objects. (You may have encountered this approach in an e-mail message from a company you have never heard of, and it includes a link to opt-out from future mailings.)

To follow the example above, collecting information on your Web site, opt-out can mean several things. You can comply with the principle of *notice* by simply stating that any email address supplied may be used for marketing purposes, but this does not meet the *choice* requirement. Choice could be a box labeled "You may not contact me about special offers on related products." There is nothing to stop you leaving this unchecked by default. So the person filling out the form must specifically request that his or her information not be used. This will not please privacy advocates, but it is perhaps more honest than *pseudo-opt-in*, where "Yes" is pre-selected as the choice next to a "Use my data" check box (a practice that is particularly annoying to privacy-sensitive individuals).

The subtleties of opt-in and opt-out as they apply to emailing lists are addressed in more detail in the context of Web site privacy in Chapter 8. It is now time to look at how privacy principles have been implemented in privacy laws, which is covered in the next chapter.

CHAPTER FOUR

PRIVACY LAWS

010101101110011011111010010111001010101011011011

"I believe that the definite establishment of this right of privacy is at this time of the greatest possible moment; for, without such a right and the easy enforcement of it, civilization must deteriorate, and modesty and refinement be crushed by brutality and vulgar indecency."

—John Gilmer Speed, "The Right of Privacy," The North American Review, Volume 163, Issue 476, July 1896.

4: Privacy Laws

The preceding chapters have discussed basic privacy principles and general laws which have been applied to privacy, such as the Federal Trade Commission Act. This chapter deals with some specific privacy laws with which your Web site may be required to comply. Some of these can impose very specific demands on your Web site's design, its content, andits security provisions, not to mention its privacy policies.

Depending on your position within your organization, your responsibilities may or may not include determining which laws apply to your site. (Consultation with corporate counsel is a good idea in any event, particularly if any of the following descriptions suggest to you that specific laws may be applicable to your site—however, as I have pointed out before, this book should not be construed as legal advice). Even if your responsibilities are confined to Web site security, design, or operations, you still may want to know which laws apply and what their implications are for security, design, and operations. If you want to read about these laws in greater depth, you will find suitable links in the Sources section at the back of the book.

Children's Online Privacy Protection Act

Of the federal statutes relating to privacy, the one that currently contains the most explicit reference to Web sites is the Children's Online Privacy Protection Act of 1998, known as COPPA. You may have overlooked COPPA because you didn't think it applied to you: The primary goal of the act is to give parents control over information collected from their children online. Children are defined as being under 13 years of age, however, **even if your web site is not directed at children, you need to be aware of the fine print in COPPA**.

As with many federal laws, COPPA comes in two forms, the legislation passed by Congress, and the rule or rules written to implement the legislation. In the case of COPPA, the law required the Federal Trade Commission to write the rule and enforce it. The scope of the COPPA rule is operators of commercial Web sites and online services that are directed to children and that collect personal information from children, **plus operators of general audience sites with actual knowledge that they are collecting information from children**. The second part of this scope statement bears repeating: "general audience sites with actual knowledge that they are collecting information from children." Clearly this could be interpreted very broadly and the implications are discussed later in the section "COPPA Implications."

The primary source for information about COPPA is the FTC Web site, which has a special section called Kidz Privacy. If you are not a parent or not otherwise in touch with issues surrounding the use of the Internet by children, you may have missed the emergence of child-specific privacy pages on Web sites. These can be seen on many of the leading Internet portals, such as MSN, AOL, and Yahoo. In Figure 4-1 you can see the main page of the FTC Kidz Privacy site.

Whatever your personal views about children using the Internet, as a business you need to be aware of the issues surrounding this phenomenon. You also need to know that a concerted effort is under way to educate the public, both young and old, about COPPA. Consider some of the advice that the FTC gives to children on its site.

- Look at a Web site's Privacy Policy to see how the site uses the information you give them.

- Talk about the site's Privacy Policy with your parents so that you and your parents will know what information the site collects about you and what it does with the information.

- Web sites must get your parent's permission before they collect many kinds of information from you.

- If a Web site has information about you that you and your parents don't want it to have, your parents can ask to see the information – and they can ask the Web site to delete or erase the information.

Figure 4-1: FTC Web site for Kidz Privacy

- Sites are not supposed to collect more information than they
  need about you for the activity you in which to want to participate. You should be able to participate in many activities online
  without having to give any information about yourself.

In other words, the government is being very proactive on this
topic, making an effort to ensure that both children and their
parents are aware of the privacy protection afforded by COPPA.
This effort actually extends well beyond the government. For
example, leading Internet Service Providers, such as Microsoft
MSN, go out of their way to highlight children's privacy rights. The
home page of the MSN Kids site features a prominent link to a
privacy page. Here is some of the advice found on that page:

"Most of all, we want you to have fun and stay safe while you are online! Remember to talk to your parents every time someone asks for your personal information online, even when it's a friend. Your parent will tell you when it's OK to give out your personal information. It's better to be safe than sorry, so always ask first!"

What COPPA Requires

By now you should be aware that COPPA is a very real law, with some very real penalties for sites that break it (numerous companies have had to pay fines in excess of $30,000). So, if you are an operator covered by COPAA, what does the rule say you must do? Basically, there are six requirements:

- Post clear and comprehensive privacy policies on the Web site describing your information practices for children's personal information.

- Provide notice to parents, and with limited exceptions, obtain verifiable parental consent before collecting personal information from children.

- Give parents the choice to consent to your collection and use of a child's information and at the same time allow them to forbid disclosure of that information, by you, to third parties.

- Provide parents' access to their child's personal information to review it or have it deleted.

- Give parents the opportunity to prevent further collection or use of the information.

- Maintain the confidentiality, security, and integrity of information you collect from children.

Note this last point. In essence, the law says your Web site must be secure. While this law does not apply to all Web sites, it is one more reason to take Web site security seriously. It reflects a trend in rules written to implement privacy legislation: mandating security requirements to support privacy assurances, in line with basic privacy principles. The consequences for companies that do not back up their privacy policies with adequate data protection mea-

sures can be severe and increasingly reflected in legal settlements
that include fines and other sanctions..

COPPA Implications

COPPA embodies the "minimum necessary" principle discussed in
Chapter 3. Children's Web sites are prohibited from conditioning a
child's participation in an online activity to require that the child
provide more information than is reasonably necessary to participate in that activity. This provision, along with several others, has a
direct impact on the design of sites, particularly if they are seeking
to involve children in activities.

Taken together, the COPPA requirements make a strong argument for including a privacy review as part of the development
cycle of web projects. Your company may already include security
reviews in the web development process and COPPA highlights a
set of issues common to many Web sites: the role of security versus
compliance.

For example, suppose you are responsible for the security of a
Web site that falls within COPPA. Clearly, COPPA requires you to
ensure that the information collected by the site is protected, but is
it your job to make sure that the data collected by the forms on the
site conforms to the restrictions of COPPA? The answer will vary
depending on your company's organizational structure and the
allocation of responsibilities. What the company needs to avoid is a
gap within that structure, through which compliance with legislation such as COPPA can slip. I will discuss issues surrounding
compliance strategy in more detail in Chapters 6 and 7.

What about the COPPA requirement that "general audience
Web sites with actual knowledge that they are collecting information from children" comply with COPPA? The first step in addressing this issue is to decide if your web site is "general audience" as
opposed to being directed at children. For example, most corporate
web sites designed to tell the public about the company are general
audience. Less easy to categorize are sites that tell people about
specific products or services. Even if the site is not directed at
children, they may visit it. If you are in doubt, and if the site collects
information, there are several ways to address the issue. For ex-

ample, you can add an age field to any form on your site that collects information, like this:

Birth Date

To comply with current law, .NET Passport requires a birth date.

There are several approaches to using an age field; the one you choose will probably depend upon how likely children are to use the form. This can be a tough call. For example, can you assume a form requesting product literature about hair loss treatments will only be of interest to adults? Perhaps, but what about a youngster who wants to help out a balding father?

And what about product literature for a sports car featured in the latest James Bond movie? Some readers may remember when James Bond movies were strictly for grown-ups, but times have changed and children today may well want to request the latest Aston Martin brochure. Whether or not you err on the side of caution, and include an age field on all forms that request personal information, is probably a committee decision (probably involving, at a minimum, marketing, the web design team, and corporate counsel).

As to the age field itself, you have a range of options. You can use a check box labeled "Check this box if you are under 13 years of age." You might leave it unchecked by default. You can use a pair of Yes/No radio buttons preceded by the question "Are you 13 years of age or older?." If you wish you can pre-select the Yes button. You can also use a pull-down list labeled "What year were you born?"

Honest Ages: The rule uses the term "actual knowledge." You are not, in most cases, liable if someone lies to you about their age (there may be exceptions, possibly based on state law, in areas such as pornographic content and age-controlled substances, such as tobacco and alcohol—many such sites attempt to use age verification systems that are based on something more than what the user says).

The approach you take will depend, in part, on the reasonableness of your assumption that the people submitting completed forms are adults. At the same time, you might want to explain the reason for this field on the form (this could simply be a link labeled

"Why do we ask this?" which pops up a window that provides and an swer, like this one:

Kids Passport

Children's Online Privacy Protection Act

The Children's Online Privacy Protection Act (COPPA) was passed by U.S. Congress in November 1998. COPPA requires that operators of online services or Web sites obtain parental consent prior to the collection, use, disclosure, or display of the personal information of children. The Federal Trade Commission established rules for the act's implementation, which went into effect April 21, 2000.

You should definitely consider explaining the question if you use the "Year you were born?" approach since some people consider this sensitive information. Of course, a field like this is quite a good idea on forms that are likely to be completed by children, since it may screen out a few of those who try to supply inaccurate information. Which brings up the question of what to do with age responses. Clearly your web form design will need to validate input based on the response, so that if someone does indicate they are under 13, the appropriate action is taken. This can either be redirection to a form that complies with COPPA rules for requesting information from children, or simply a response that says "Sorry, you must be 13 or older to use this form."

COPPA Safe Harbor

Regardless of who within your company is tasked with COPPA compliance, it might help to know that the FTC has approved several "safe harbor" programs for COPPA. Safe harbor programs are industry self-regulatory guidelines that, if adhered to, are deemed to implement or comply with government regulation. COPPA safe harbor is available by participating in the TRUSTe seal program. It is also available from the Entertainment Software Rating Board (ESRB) and the Children's Advertising Review Unit of the Council of Better Business Bureaus (CARU), an arm of the advertising industry's self-regulatory program.

Gramm-Leach-Bliley

Switching gears now, and flashing back to the summer of 2001, do you remember receiving stacks of letters about privacy? They were sent via "snail mail" to millions of Americans by banks and credit card companies, stock brokers and pension plans, and a whole range of miscellaneous financial institutions. These mailings were a direct result of the Financial Services Modernization Act of 1999, more commonly referred to as Gramm-Leach-Bliley or G-L-B, after the three congressmen who drafted the legislation. The main purpose of G-L-B was not privacy, but dismantling the regulation of financial services that was imposed after the Depression by the Glass-Steagall Act of 1933.

Under G-L-B, financial services providers, including banks, securities firms and insurance companies, can affiliate with each other and enter each other's markets—the goal being open and free competition in the financial services industry. However, during the drafting of the legislation, a lot of people expressed concern over the sharing of information between different types of companies, such as insurers and bankers, who would have new opportunities to "cross-sell" under G-L-B that they did not have under Glass-Steagall. The section of G-L-B that most directly affects Web sites is titled "Disclosure of Nonpublic Personal Information." This section states that

> "Each financial institution has an affirmative and continuing obligation to respect the privacy of its customers.... A financial institution has an affirmative and continuing obligation to protect the security and confidentiality of its customers' nonpublic personal information."

G-L-B Definitions

How is "nonpublic personal information" defined? Quite broadly, . Nonpublic personal information is personally identifiable financial information that is provided by a consumer to a financial institution, the results from any transaction with the consumer or any financial service performed for the consumer, or information otherwise obtained by the financial institution. Examples of "nonpublic personal information" include:

- information a consumer provides on an application to obtain a loan or open an account;

- account balance information, payment history and credit card information;

- the fact that an individual is or has been one of your customers or has obtained a financial product or service from your company;

- any information that a consumer provides to your company or an agent of your company;

- information otherwise obtained in connection with collecting on or servicing a credit account.

In terms of restrictions on the use of nonpublic personal information, G-L-B prohibits financial institutions from disclosing it to a nonaffiliated third party (either directly or through an affiliate), unless the institution has:

- disclosed to the consumer, in a clear and conspicuous manner, that the information might be disclosed to such third party;

- given the consumer an opportunity to direct that the information not be disclosed; and

- described the manner in which the consumer can exercise the nondisclosure option.

The basic implication for Web sites is the same as with COPPA: when the data handled by the site is of a type that is covered by the legislation, protection of the data is required by law. In fact, G-L-B has created security standards that financial institutions must meet when handling nonpublic personal information (links to these can be found in the Sources section at the back of the book).

Bear in mind that G-L-B does not just apply to banks and insurance companies. The law defines "Financial Institution" broadly, including any entity that engages in activities that are "financial in nature" and virtually any other financial activity that federal regulators may designate. This encompasses entities such as mortgage lenders and brokers, check-cashing services, wire transfer services, travel agencies operated in connection with financial services, debt collectors, credit counselors, financial advisors, tax preparation firms, car dealers, and more.

G-L-B and Pretexting

A separate part of the legislation specifically outlaws obtaining nonpublic personal information through deception (a practice often referred to as *pretexting*, such as impersonating a customer to access personal information). A classic pretexting scenario is the private investigator hired by one spouse to find the assets of the other during a divorce. The PI telephones the target's bank and "spoofs" the target's identity, for example, using knowledge of their account number and maiden name to ascertain bank balance information, or identifying themselves by the name of the target's supposed fiancé (a tactic used by FTC investigators who ran a successful sting operation against professional pretexters in 2001).

The idea of a PI finagling PII over the phone might strike Web site operators as very low-tech, but hundreds of people suffer privacy violations every day because of such tactics. Until the passage of G-L-B, prosecuting perpetrators of such acts was difficult. Now, as the FTC has shown, it is relatively easy. Analogous behavior takes place on the Web and it is reasonable to expect that attempts to gain unauthorized access to protected information via sites will increase, particularly since the perceived risk of getting caught in "cyber-space" is considerably less than in the real world Readers who count Web site security among their responsibilities may note that G-L-B offers an interesting avenue of prosecution against those who attempt to circumvent access controls by supplying fraudulent information, such as someone else's name and password—although federal wire fraud charges might work just as well, under U.S. Code, Title 18, Part I, Chapter 63, Sec. 134.

G-L-B Implications

Any organization that comes under G-L-B is required to determine its policies and practices with respect to privacy, specifically in the following areas:

- disclosures of nonpublic personal information to affiliates and nonaffiliated third parties;

- disclosures of nonpublic personal information of persons who have ceased to be customers of the institution;

- the categories of nonpublic personal information the institution collects;

- and the protections provided to assure the confidentiality and security of nonpublic personal information.

G-L-B mandates the implementation of a comprehensive written information security program that includes administrative, technical, and physical safeguards for customer records and information appropriate to the size and complexity of the organization and the nature and scope of its activities. The organization's board of directors, or an appropriate committee of the board, must approve and oversee the development, implementation, and maintenance of the information security program. And the organization is

---

Privacy Challenge: Management decides that the company's Web site needs to be upgraded to allow customers to order products and pay by credit card. What are the privacy implications? Does the addition of credit card payment processing require that your site be G-L-B compliant? What other privacy laws may apply to your site if you add this feature?

First, you present these questions to corporate counsel so that you will have a formal and up-to-date opinion on file to document any privacy-related design decisions you make. You will probably be informed that accepting credit card payments alone does not bring your company under G-L-B. However, if you were to offer phased payments, where a portion of the purchase price for an expensive item is billed to the customer's card in installments, there may be a G-L-B implication.

Regardless of G-L-B implications, you will want to update your Web site's privacy statement to reflect the collection of personal information, such as billing address and phone number, necessary to process credit card payments. You may wish to assure shoppers that such information will not be sold to third parties or used for marketing purposes without their explicit permission, which, if given, can be revoked at any time.

And of course, you will want to make sure the site's security measures are adequate to protect credit card information during transmission, processing, and storage.

---

required to exercise appropriate due diligence in selecting and monitoring service providers, who must implement appropriate security measures to meet the objectives of the guidelines. In other words, if you are responsible for any Web sites belonging to organizations in the financial field, or even to companies servicing such organizations, appropriate security for those sites may be required by law.

G-L-B Response

Unfortunately, recitations of the law can give the impression that the audience is somehow assumed to be guilty, but nobody is suggesting that the operators of Web sites which handle personal financial data, are somehow lacking in concern for the privacy and security of said data. The point here is that the concern is now mandated and the letter of the law, not just its spirit, must now be observed. So, if you operate a Web site that handles personal financial data, your first response to first hearing about G-L-B should be to learn more. Familiarize yourself with the regulations and determine whether or not your company is covered by them.

An area of particular relevance to Web site operations is the "downstream" use of data. In other words, if users of the site input nonpublic personal information, then you need to know whether or not it is later disclosed to either affiliates or nonaffiliated third parties. Notice of such disclosures is required and permission to make them needs to be obtained. The site's privacy statement should indicate the categories of nonpublic personal information the site collects, and describe, in general terms, the protections provided to assure its confidentiality and security.

Health Insurance Portability and Accountability Act

Do not be tempted to skip this section if your Web site has nothing to do with health insurance. The legislation commonly referred to as HIPAA covers a lot more data than the name might suggest. If your Web site is even loosely related to medicine, doctors, insurance, pharmaceuticals, or anything remotely health-oriented, you should read this section. What you do about HIPAA beyond that will depend, first of all, upon whether or not HIPAA applies to your site. Making such a determination can be difficult. The whole of HIPAA is thousands of pages long. The part about privacy takes up 1,500 pages (in some double-spaced versions). One sub-part of the definition of "covered entity" has 13 sections (covered entity being the collective noun for organizations that must comply with HIPAA, although HIPAA also affects organizations classified as "business associates" and "hybrid entities").

So if your reading of this section does not give you a clear answer as to whether or not your Web site is covered by HIPAA, please consult the references in the Sources section at the end of the book. I am not saying this to pass the buck. The fact is, no single document, however long, can possibly answer— for every permutation of company, product, service, or situation—the simple, three-word question I have been asked at seminar after seminar: "Are we covered?"

What is HIPAA?

Many consumers know of HIPAA from when it was passed as the Kennedy-Kassebaum Act in 1996, but it was not associated with privacy back then. The goal of the act was to make it easier for people to keep health insurance coverage when they change jobs. So how did we get from there to "the first-ever comprehensive federal regulation that gives patients sweeping protections over the privacy of their medical records," which is how Secretary of Health and Human Services, Tommy G. Thompson, announced the final version of the HIPAA Privacy Rule in August of 2002?

The short version goes like this: The framers of the legislation, Senators Kennedy and Kassebaum, realized that it would increase the cost of health insurance—for example, by limiting the ability of insurers to deny claims or coverage due to pre-existing conditions— so to offset this, the law attempted to encourage a trend toward cost-saving computerization of medical records, notably in the area of billing and payment. In the early nineties there were numerous studies that suggested standardization of billing codes could generate enormous financial benefits to insurers and healthcare providers, notably in terms of faster, more accurate payments with fewer clerical staff requirements and less fraud. Unfortunately, early industry efforts at voluntary standardization had failed, so HIPAA imposed them, in a section of the law referred to as—no sarcasm, puns or irony intended—"Administrative Simplification."

The reason your Web site might be affected by HIPAA is that within the Administrative Simplification section, lawmakers addressed the potential loss of privacy associated with increased use of computerized medical data. Lawmakers also gave themselves the option of drafting the rules that implement the legislation, but handed this task to the Department of Health and Human Services (HHS). So HHS went through an extensive draft-publish-comment-finalize process for numerous rules, including a Privacy Rule and a Security Rule.

Under the Privacy Rule, a category of personal information called Individually Identifiable Health Information is defined, together with a sub-category: Protected Health Information or PHI. Those organizations or entities that are covered by the legislation are forbidden to use or disclose protected health information, except in the specific circumstances laid out in the rule. With respect to the handling of PHI, the Privacy Rule states:

> "A covered entity must have in place appropriate administrative, technical, and physical safeguards to protect the privacy of protected health information."

This puts everyone on notice that, within a wide range of specified circumstances, privacy protection for health information is the law; but it does not give much guidance on what constitutes "appropriate safeguards." This is spelled out in a separate Security Rule that attempts to "define the security requirements to be fulfilled to preserve health information confidentiality and privacy as defined in the law."

The compliance deadline for the Privacy Rule was set at April 14, 2003, but a compliance deadline for the Security Rule had not been set even as late as eight months before that date. However, the position of HHS has always been that the security measures described in the proposed version of the Security Rule were no more than industry best practices, things that a responsible organization should already be doing. Ask any security professional to read the proposed Security Rule and they will probably agree. Unfortunately, it is hard to find anyone who agrees with the statement that security practices in the health care industry, circa 2002, are close to where they should be. In my personal and professional experience, the average bank or brokerage has far better information security policies and practices than the average health care company.

Individually Identifiable Health Information means any information, including demographic information, collected from an individual, that—
a. Is created or received by a health care provider, health plan, employer, or health care clearinghouse; and
b. Relates to the past, present or future physical or mental health or condition of an individual, the provision of health care to an individual, or the past, present, or future payment for the provision of health care to an individual, and
(i) Identifies the individual, or
ii) With respect to which there is a reasonable basis to believe that the information can be used to identify the individual.

The proposed Security Rule mandates safeguards for physical storage and maintenance, transmission, and access to individual health information. Although the final version of the rule may modify its scope, my reading of the proposed version is that its application will be broad, potentially encompassing all individual health information that is electronically maintained or transmitted (by a health care provider, health plan, public health authority, employer, life insurer, school or university, or health care clearinghouse). Fortunately, the Security Rule does not require specific technologies to be used. It is assumed solutions will vary from business to business, depending on factors such as the size of the organization, its location, and technologies in use.

Web Site Implications

The HIPAA Privacy Rule affects all healthcare organizations, including care providers, health plans, physician offices, employers, public health authorities, life insurers, medical payment clearinghouses, medical billing agencies, medical information systems vendors, medical service organizations and universities. The Privacy Rule mandates protection for the privacy of information related to an individual's health, treatment, or healthcare payment. The Privacy Rule gives individuals the right to receive written notice of information practices and to access and amend their health information. Plans and providers also have to provide an audit trail of health information disclosures and get individuals' written authorization for use of their information for purposes other than treatment, payment, or healthcare operations. Organizations must also limit the information disclosed to the minimum amount necessary.

For Web sites, the implications of HIPAA are much the same as those of the fair information practice principles. **Notice** must be provided if visitors are inputting health information at your site (that notice will need to be HIPAA compliant). Visitors must be given a **choice** about providing health information and an explanation of the implications of not supplying the information. **Permission** to use individually identifiable health information will be needed; sometimes very specific permission language will be needed to comply with HIPAA.

Adequate measures to **protect** health information must be taken. When health information is submitted to a Web site, or displayed by a Web site, it must be encrypted in transit both ways. The widely used SSL protocol can meet this requirement however, unless the client has a valid digital certificate installed, SSL alone cannot perform strong authentication—encrypting the PHI you send to someone's browser does not make it secure unless you take adequate steps to reliably identify that someone.

If your site receives any PHI you must **protect** it during processing, storage, and possible onward transmission. Typically, this means not storing it on the Web server itself, but on a properly firewalled back-end system. An encrypted database application with strong user authentication and granular access controls is strongly indicated, particularly since someone, although possibly not the Web site operator, needs to be able to **account** for all accesses to PHI.

You may be called upon to provide, via the Web site, **access** by individuals to their information, but you should approach this with caution. Unless you can implement strong authentication, it will be difficult to guarantee that you are providing access to the appropriate person, which raises the prospect of unauthorized disclosures. It may well be that traditional methods, such as paper forms presented in person, will need to be used.

Policies and procedures for handling PHI will need to be in place and documented. One important element to include: consequences for those who violate the policies. People will need to be taught what the policies and procedures are and how to comply with them. This training requirement is not only stressed throughout HIPAA, but also emphasized in FTC privacy settlements, suggesting it is one area where your company can protect itself through due diligence. In other words, your company can prevent or reduce punishment for alleged privacy violations by showing that a good faith effort was made to prevent them.

Last, but not least, if your Web site handles PHI, someone within your organization must be appointed to be responsible for privacy. Like training, this requirement is part of HIPAA and strongly echoed in FTC privacy settlements. Furthermore, it is a consistent theme in international privacy guidelines, because it goes to the **enforcement** of privacy protection.

A Fine Thing: If you are having trouble getting management to pay attention to HIPAA, you might point out that the law calls for severe civil and criminal penalties for noncompliance, including fines up to $25K for multiple violations of the same standard in a calendar year, even if they are not intentional. Illegal sale of individually identifiable health information carries fines up to $250,000 and/or imprisonment up to 10 years.

Broader Implications

If you work in the health care field, you already know that HIPAA has created its own industry, from IT overhauls to handle the transaction code set implementations, to gap analysis and policy generation for compliance with the Privacy Rule. There are several broad implications for Web sites. When early versions of the Privacy Rule appeared, some IT vendors took an extreme view of its implications and scope in order to scare up business. When the Privacy Rule was revised in 2002, some of the extremes simply went away. This led some people to discount vendor claims completely, despite the fact that part of what they had been saying remained true. At the same time, a looming compliance deadline (April 14, 2003) led a lot of organizations to focus on meeting the letter of the law. In some cases this happened at the expense of broader thinking about privacy in those organizations.

Health Privacy is Not About HIPAA Compliance

The biggest health privacy case so far this century is the Prozac Email Incident. Although the company involved, Eli Lilly, only paid $160,000 in fines, the total cost of settling was considerably more, and is ongoing. That case had nothing to do with HIPAA and neither did high profile cases from last century such as the Tammy Wynette medical privacy incident, which resulted in both tort action and federal wire fraud charges. In other words, it would be a mistake for health-related organizations to focus too much attention on whether or not, or in what way, they must meet the requirements of the HIPAA Privacy Rule.

If you are covered, you must comply. But you must also do more than merely comply, in order to avoid incidents or situations that lead to damaging tort- or FTCA-based actions. If you are not covered by HIPAA, and don't have to comply with the Privacy Rule, it would be a mistake to think that your privacy obligations are any less than if you had to. The bottom line for both covered and non-covered organizations is that HIPAA will raise expectations of privacy protection for all personal health-related information, and provide a standard against which privacy promises and protections can be judged.

Sad Song: When headlines in the National Enquirer declared that country singer Tammy Wynette needed a liver transplant to save her life, the information was not only incorrect, it was obtained illegally, from an employee at Pittsburgh University Medical Center. The singer sued the National Enquirer, citing a loss of earnings due to bookings being cancelled by venues fearful she would be too sick to perform. While a judge threw out her claim of libel, he upheld her right of tort action for privacy invasion. The tabloid settled out of court for an undisclosed sum and the man who faxed the singer's medical records to supermarket tabloids—in return for $2,610—later pleaded guilty to a federal charge of wire fraud and was sentenced to six months' confinement.

Training, Training, Training

The combined training requirements of the HIPAA privacy and security rules make it abundantly clear that failure to adequately educate appropriate personnel on the proper care and handling of individually identifiable health information will be judged as negligence. This was underscored by the FTC's decisions in both the Microsoft Passport and Eli Lilly Prozac cases. The implication for organizations that operate Web sites that handle personal information is obvious: staff must be given privacy training. Giving proper privacy training to the people who code pages that handle personal data cannot guarantee the elimination of errors or abuses leading to privacy violations; but it can guarantee a strong defense for the organization if it gets hauled into court. That defense goes something like this:

> "Your Honor, we deeply regret this incident but do not feel our company should be held responsible for its occurrence. The person responsible, an employee in our IT department, had been given extensive privacy training specifically designed to prevent such an incident. The HR records we have submitted to the court show the exact date on which he completed the course and a certificate of completion was issued."

Other Laws

Privacy law has been discussed in various contexts in each of the three preceding chapters. The tort basis for privacy rights and privacy actions was addressed in Chapter 1. The Federal Trade Commission Act was introduced in Chapter 2, while Chapter 3 described the Privacy Act. This chapter has focused on the three most recent U.S. privacy laws: COPPA, G-L-B, and HIPPA. There is simply not enough room here to cover the more than thirty other Federal laws that affect privacy in some way:

1. Administrative Procedure Act. (5 U.S.C. §§ 551, 554-558)
2. Cable Communications Policy Act (47 U.S.C. § 551)
3. Census Confidentiality Statute (13 U.S.C. § 9)
4. Children's Online Privacy Protection Act of 1998 (15 U.S.C. §§ 6501 et seq., 16

C.F.R. § 312)
5. Communications Assistance for Law Enforcement (47 U.S.C. § 1001)
6. Computer Security Act (40 U.S.C. § 1441)
7. Criminal Justice Information Systems (42 U.S.C. § 3789g)
8. Customer Proprietary Network Information (47 U.S.C. § 222)
9. Driver's Privacy Protection Act (18 U.S.C. § 2721)
10. Drug and Alcoholism Abuse Confidentiality Statutes (21 U.S.C. § 1175; 42 U.S.C. § 290dd-3)
11. Electronic Communications Privacy Act (18 U.S.C. § 2701, et seq.)
12. Electronic Funds Transfer Act (15 U.S.C. § 1693, 1693m)
13. Employee Polygraph Protection Act (29 U.S.C. § 2001, et seq.)
14. Employee Retirement Income Security Act (29 U.S.C. § 1025)
15. Equal Credit Opportunity Act (15 U.S.C. § 1691, et. seq.)
16. Equal Employment Opportunity Act (42 U.S.C. § 2000e, et seq.)
17. Fair Credit Billing Act (15 U.S.C. § 1666)
18. Fair Credit Reporting Act (15 U.S.C. § 1681 et seq.)
19. Fair Debt Collection Practices Act (15 U.S.C. § 1692 et seq.)
20. Fair Housing Statute (42 U.S, C. §§ 3604, 3605)
21. Family Educational Rights and Privacy Act (20 U.S.C. § 1232g)
22. Freedom of Information Act (5 U.S.C. § 552) (FOIA)
23. Gramm-Leach-Bliley Act (15 U.S.C. §§ 6801 et seq)
24. Health Insurance Portability and Accountability Act (Pub. Law No. 104-191 §§ 262,264: 45 C.F.R. §§ 160-164)
25. Health Research Data Statute (42 U.S.C. § 242m)
26. Mail Privacy Statute (39 U.S.C. § 3623)
27. Paperwork Reduction Act of 1980 (44 U.S.C. § 3501, et seq.)
28. Privacy Act (5 U.S.C. § 552a)
29. Privacy Protection Act (42 U.S.C. § 2000aa)
30. Right to Financial Privacy Act (12 U.S.C. § 3401, et seq.)
31. Tax Reform Act (26 U.S.C. §§ 6103, 6108, 7609)
32. Telephone Consumer Protection Act (47 U.S.C. § 227)
33. Video Privacy Protection Act (18 U.S.C. § 2710)
34. Wiretap Statutes (18 U.S.C. § 2510, et seq.; 47 U.S.C. § 605)

The good news is, the laws in the above list that have a direct bearing on Web site privacy for businesses have now been covered. If you are interested in the others, you will find them referenced in the Sources section of www.privacyforbusiness.com.

CHAPTER FIVE

PRIVACY LAWS WORLDWIDE

010101101110011011111010010111001010101011011011

"To prevent abuses of personal data and ensure that data subjects are informed of the existence of processing operations, the Directive lays down common rules, to be observed by those who collect, hold or transmit personal data as part of their economic or administrative activities or in the course of the activities of their association. In particular, there is an obligation to collect data only for specified, explicit and legitimate purposes, and to be held only if it is relevant, accurate and up-to-date."

—European Union Press Release on the EU Data Protection Directive 95/46/EC, July 25, 1995.

5: PRIVACY LAWS WORLDWIDE

O ne of the easiest things to forget when you are designing or managing a Web site is the meaning of the "WWW" in your URL. Of course, everyone knows WWW stands for World Wide Web, and most people understand that a public Web site on the Internet is visible to everyone else on the Internet. What people tend to forget is that no amount of targeting in the design and promotion of a web site will ensure it is only visited by a particular audience. If it is on the Internet, it is visible to anyone else who is on the Internet, from Alaska to Zimbabwe. Does this mean you need to know all the privacy laws in all the jurisdictions in all the countries of the world? Probably not, but unless your company actively discourages any contact with the world beyond the border, some-body involved with the Web site should have some basic under-standing of privacy laws outside your country. Providing that understanding is the goal of this chapter.

Global Considerations

Earlier chapters have tended to assume that your company Web site is located in the United States and this chapter will continue that assumption, presenting privacy laws from other countries to a largely American audience. However, this chapter will also echo the book's international bias: business Web sites need, for good business reasons, to be cognizant of privacy practices in countries other than the ones in which they are located. Of course, not all of the world's privacy laws are covered here. Instead, the main focus is on one particular non-U.S. example, the European Union, or E.U. This approach not only serves to cover many countries at once; it also provides insight into an attitude to data privacy that is very differ-ent from the one prevalent in the United States. Beyond this, and in recognition of the fact that the United States and the European

Union represent just a handful of the countries that are on the Internet, references to privacy laws in additional countries are provided in the Sources section at the back of the book.

Public Web Site was used on purpose in the first paragraph of this chapter. As pointed out in Chapter 1, this is really another term for "normal Web site," one that is accessible to anyone on the Internet, as opposed to a "nonpublic" Web site, access to which is restricted to a group of known persons. There is probably no need for nonpublic Web sites to be concerned with localized privacy notices. However, if such sites are part of an international company intranet, one which enables transborder data flows, then there are definitely privacy issues that the company will need to address.

One other global consideration is the localization of site content and privacy policies. This is particularly challenging for companies that have or want business in multiple countries. Consider companies like Epson or Canon, which sell products worldwide. Go to epson.com or canon.com and the first thing you see is a world map, so that visitors can get to sites that are specific to their location. If you go to Canon's U.S. site you will find a privacy statement that is U.S. specific. Go to the Canon site for the United Kingdom and privacy is handled differently. However, this approach has not been universally adopted and no real standard has emerged in this area since commerce on the Web is still such a recent phenomenon (only 8 years old if you date the commercial Web from 1994, which is when amazon.com opened).

Data Protection in the E.U.

The European Union is a geographic, economic, and political entity currently composed of 15 member countries: Austria, Belgium, Denmark, Finland, France, Germany, Greece, Ireland, Italy, Luxembourg, The Netherlands, Portugal, Spain, Sweden, and the United Kingdom. For those unfamiliar with the European Union, or unclear as to why its privacy policies could be of importance, you should note that the total population of the European Union is greater than all of North America and its membership encompasses 10 of the world's 15 richest nations.

As far back as the 1980s, some members of the European Union were creating data privacy legislation modeled after the principles and guidelines described earlier in this chapter, establishing some fundamental protections for data subjects. For example, the United Kingdom passed the Data Protection Act in 1984, which addressed the Enforcement/Redress principle by establishing the office of Data Protection Commissioner, with whom all data controllers must register. A *data controller* is defined as anyone who determines the purposes for which and the manner in which any personal data are, or are to be, processed; in broad terms, anyone who has a database containing information about people. This publicly accessible registry lists the name and address of the data controller and a general description of the processing of personal data performed by the data controller. Individuals can consult the register to find out what processing of personal data is being carried out by a particular data controller. (The UK Data Protection Act was substantially updated in 1998, but it stuck to this database registration approach, which conveniently illustrates the extent to which the European and American approaches differ.)

The E.U. Data Protection Directive

While members of the European Union are free to create their own laws, they also have an obligation to harmonize those laws within the Union. Hence the Data Protection Directive (DPD) which was passed in 1995 to harmonize data protection laws. The DPD went into effect in 1998, not only setting common standards for protection of data across the European Union, but also establishing "the fundamental rights and freedoms of natural persons, and in particular their right to privacy, with respect to the processing of personal data." Under the DPD personal data must be:

- Processed fairly and lawfully

- Collected for specified, explicit, and legitimate purposes

- Adequate, relevant, and not excessive in relation to the purposes for which they are collected

- Accurate and, where necessary, kept up to date

- Kept in a form that permits identification of data subjects for no longer than is necessary for the purposes for which the data were collected or for which they are further processed

If you have read Chapter 2, you will recognize the above as a restatement of well-established data privacy principles. However, the DPD also stipulates that:

"the transfer to a third country of personal data which are undergoing processing or are intended for processing after transfer may take place only if...the country in question ensures an adequate level of protection."

In other words, the DPD prohibits the transfer of data relating to individuals to non-E.U. countries that are considered "unsafe" destinations for protection of personal data. Based on what you have read in previous chapters, it should not come as a surprise that the United States is considered, by the European Union, to be "unsafe." Here is a diplomatic statement of the situation from the Web site of the U.S. Department of Commerce.

"While the United States and the European Union share the goal of enhancing privacy protection for their citizens, the United States takes a different approach to privacy from that taken by the European Union. The United States uses a sectoral approach that relies on a mix of legislation, regulation, and self-regulation. The European Union, however, relies on comprehensive legislation that, for example, requires creation of government data protection agencies, registration of data bases with those agencies, and in some instances prior approval before personal data processing may begin."

In fact, the E.U. and the U.S. have had some pretty robust exchanges on this topic, which make for interesting reading if you are interested in the topic of international perspectives on privacy. The U.S. Department of Commerce Web site is diplomatic when it says:

"As a result of these different privacy approaches, the Directive could have significantly hampered the ability of U.S. companies to engage in many trans-Atlantic transactions."

In other words, the Directive implied that the ability of American companies to move data from Europe into the U.S. would face serious obstacles. Fortunately, as described in the next section, serious trade negotiations and diplomatic activities prevented a "data war" from erupting between Europe and America.

U.S./E.U. Safe Harbor

The U.S. Department of Commerce was able to bridge these two different privacy approaches by negotiating a streamlined means for U.S. organizations to comply with the DPD. In consultation with the European Commission, the Department of Commerce developed a Safe Harbor framework that was approved by the E.U. in July 2000. The department's Web site describes this as:

> "An important way for U.S. companies to avoid experiencing interruptions in their business dealings with the E.U. or facing prosecution by European authorities under European privacy laws. Certifying to the safe harbor will assure that E.U. organizations know that your company provides "adequate" privacy protection, as defined by the Directive."

Before getting into the details of Safe Harbor, it should be noted that Safe Harbor is not necessary in two situations: when the data subject consents to the transfer, or when the transferor commits to "adequate safeguards" for the treatment of the data in the receiving country through a contract between transferor and transferee. Both of these exceptions can be used to keep data flowing into the U.S. from the E.U.

Both make sense in a number of situations. For example, adding DPD compliant language to a contract when an American company is contracting with a European company for data processing services, or vice versa, is relatively convenient (the Department of Commerce Web site for Safe Harbor actually provides a model contract). In terms of web site operations, getting permission from European data subjects to process their data in the U.S. can be achieved through a suitable "Click to Agree" field adjacent to a disclosure statement on a data entry form.

Any U.S. company certifying its privacy practices to the Safe Harbor can satisfy E.U. organizations that the company provides "adequate" privacy protection, as defined by the directive. To qualify, an American company agrees to seven Safe Harbor principles, reproduced here because they represent a useful restatement of basic privacy principles.

1. Notice

An organization must inform individuals about the purposes for which it collects and uses information about them, how to contact the organization with any inquiries or complaints, the types of third parties to which it discloses the information, and the choices and means the organization offers individuals for limiting its use and disclosure. This notice must be provided in clear and conspicuous language when individuals are first asked to provide personal information to the organization or as soon thereafter as is practicable, and certainly before the organization uses such information for a purpose other than that for which it was originally collected or processed by the transferring organization or discloses it for the first time to a third party.

2. Choice

An organization must offer individuals the opportunity to choose (opt out) whether their personal information is (a) to be disclosed to a third party or (b) to be used for a purpose that is incompatible with the purpose(s) for which it was originally collected or subsequently authorized by the individual. Individuals must be provided with clear and conspicuous, readily available, and affordable mechanisms to exercise choice.

For sensitive information (i.e. personal information specifying medical or health conditions, racial or ethnic origin, political opinions, religious or philosophical beliefs, trade union membership or information specifying the sex life of the individual), they must be given affirmative or explicit (opt in) choice if the information is to be disclosed to a third party or used for a purpose other than those for which it was originally collected or subsequently authorized by the individual through the exercise of opt in choice. In any case, an organization should treat as sensitive any information received from a third party where the third party treats and identifies it as sensitive.

3. Onward Transfer

To disclose information to a third party, organizations must apply the Notice and Choice Principles. Where an organization wishes to transfer information to a third party that is acting as an agent, as described in the endnote, it may do so if it first either ascertains that the third party subscribes to the Principles or is subject to the Directive or another adequacy finding or enters into a written agreement with such third party requiring that the third party provide at least the same level of privacy protection as is required by the relevant Principles. If the organization complies with these requirements it shall not be held responsible (unless the organization agrees otherwise) when a third party to which it transfers such information, processes it in a way contrary to any restrictions or representations, unless the organization knew or should have known the third party would process it in such a contrary way and the organization has not taken reasonable steps to prevent or stop such processing.

4. Security

Organizations creating, maintaining, using or disseminating personal information must take reasonable precautions to protect it from loss, misuse and unauthorized access, disclosure, alteration and destruction.

5. Data Integrity

Consistent with the Principles, personal information must be relevant for the purposes for which it is to be used. An organization may not process personal information in a way that is incompatible with the purposes for which it has been collected or subsequently authorized by the individual. To the extent necessary for those purposes, an organization should take reasonable steps to ensure that data is reliable for its intended use, accurate, complete, and current.

6. Access

Individuals must have access to personal information about them that an organization holds and be able to correct, amend, or delete that information where it is inaccurate, except where the burden or expense of providing access would be disproportionate to the risks to the individual's privacy in the case in question, or where the rights of persons other than the individual would be violated.

7. Enforcement

Effective privacy protection must include mechanisms for assuring compliance with the Principles, recourse for individuals to whom the data relate affected by non-compliance with the Principles, and consequences for the organization when the Principles are not followed. At a minimum, such mechanisms must include

a) readily available and affordable independent recourse mechanisms by which each individual's complaints and disputes are investigated and resolved by reference to the Principles and damages awarded where the applicable law or private sector initiatives so provide;

b) follow up procedures for verifying that the attestations and assertions businesses make about their privacy practices are true and that privacy practices have been implemented as presented; and

c) obligations to remedy problems arising out of failure to comply with the Principles by organizations announcing their adherence to them and consequences for such organizations. Sanctions must be sufficiently rigorous to ensure compliance by organizations.

The seven numbered sections above are taken more or less verbatim from the Safe Harbor section of Department of Commerce Web site (www.export.gov/safeharbor). This site provides extensive background on the program, a compliance workbook, all the necessary forms, and hosts the list of companies that have certified. Note that companies certify themselves; they are not certified by the Department of Commerce. While this approach has been criticized by some privacy advocates, the fact remains that all 15 Member States of the European Union are bound by the European Commission's finding of adequacy for the Safe Harbor program. In this context, adequacy means a level of privacy protection sufficient to allow data to be transferred out of the E.U. and into the certified entity. Companies participating in the safe harbor will be deemed adequate and data flows to those companies will continue. Furthermore, claims brought by European citizens against U.S. companies will be heard in the U.S. subject to limited exceptions.

The Value of Safe Harbor

E.U. Safe Harbor has been used effectively by some U.S. companies as both a justification and an incentive to raise privacy standards. The argument goes like this:

1. E.U. privacy standards are a barrier to business in a very big market unless we:

    a. Obtain special privacy consents for Europeans;

    b. Create special contracts for anything that involves European PII; or

    c. Certify our privacy policies and procedures to certain standards.

2. We already know that we need to create/overhaul our privacy policies and procedures regardless of E.U. issues.

3. We can gain significant business advantage if we have independent verification of our privacy policies and procedures, or other evidence that they meet certain standards.

4. Certifying to E.U. Safe Harbor gives us a standard to which we can work, and privacy bragging rights when we get there.

However important you think privacy is to your company, when it comes to resources, privacy is one issue among many. By showing that a privacy initiative accomplishes multiple goals you stand a better chance of getting more of the resources you need.

Other Safe Harbors

The concept of Safe Harbor was mentioned earlier in the context of COPPA. Several organizations—TRUSTe, for example—have been approved by the FTC to offer Safe Harbor for COPPA. Regulators currently favor such programs as a means of bringing additional resources and oversight to bear on compliance issues.

In fact, TRUSTe has been approved by the Commerce Department to offer safe harbor for E.U. Safe Harbor. By working with TRUSTe, which your company may be doing already because of the TRUSTe Privacy Seal on its Web Site, you can streamline and simplify compliance with E.U. requirements. Clearly, there is the potential to cover a lot of bases by working with TRUSTe, but you cannot simply buy compliance by paying the licensing fee—you must do all that is necessary to comply with TRUSTe's requirements, as discussed in Chapter 9.

CHAPTER SIX

POLICIES, NOTICES AND STATEMENTS

010101101110011011111010010111001010101011011011

"In this increasingly complex world, even legitimate businesses will suffer when consumers' perceptions of the control and safety of their personal information online are damaged. Companies should clearly and pervasively communicate their policies on data gathering and use of data to make trade-offs between information and benefits increasingly clear to consumers."

—Rob Leathern, Jupiter Research analyst, March, 2002

6: POLICIES, NOTICES AND STATEMENTS

Although privacy statements have become an integral part of Web site design, as noted in Chapter 1, a privacy statement is much more than a design element. Your company's Web site privacy statement **must** be based on policies to which your company is committed. This implies a considerable amount of corporate decision-making, which in turn implies a corporate strategy with respect to privacy. Such a strategy must include more than what you say about privacy; it must cover what you do, including what you do when things go wrong. The goal of this chpater, and the one that follows, is to help you develop your company's privacy strategy, to address privacy policies, privacy practices, and privacy incident response.

Privacy Disclosures

Visit just about any popular Web site and you will find a privacy disclosure of some kind. Often this is a link on the home page that contains the word *privacy* and leads to a statement of the Web site's privacy practices. Such statements are sometimes referred to as notices, in keeping with the first principle of fair information practice principles, which is Notice. Whether they are called statements or notices or policies, such disclosures are almost universal now on company Web sites.

An in-depth survey conducted by Ernst and Young at the end of 2001 found that close to 100 percent of the 85 most popular sites on the Web provided at least one privacy disclosure. A site was deemed to make a privacy disclosure if it posted a privacy policy—defined as a "comprehensive description of a domain's information practices"—or made an information practice statement—defined as "a discrete statement that describes a particular practice regarding consumers' personal information."

In addition, and perhaps of more importance to the majority of mainstream companies, the same survey found that 8 out of 10 randomly selected Web sites also provided privacy disclosures. This was a considerable increase from the findings a year earlier when a similar study by the Federal Trade Commission found less than two thirds of a similar sample posted privacy disclosures. Clearly, the practice has been widely adopted, even though no universal legal requirement for such disclosures currently exists.

However, there *is* a universal legal requirement that privacy disclosures be accurate. Early chapters have made reference to FTC enforcement of "privacy promises" in the United States as well as similar thinking in other countries, such as Australia, where the Australian Competition and Consumer Commission works with the Federal Privacy Commissioner to ensure that privacy statements issued by companies are not misleading or deceptive. This means that simply posting a privacy notice on your Web site is not enough, it has to be reflected in the way that the organization does business.

Statement, Notice or Policy?

You may be wondering what differences there are, if any, between privacy policies, notices, and statements. The main distinction is between privacy policies on the one hand and notices/statements on the other. You can use privacy notice and privacy statement interchangeably, but there is a good case for saying they are not the same as privacy policy.

Ideally, a privacy statement or notice on a Web site will say how the site implements the company's overall privacy policy, particularly with respect to Web-related data such as cookies, Web bugs, Web beacons, visitor tracking, email addresses, and so on. If you want to refer to this as "the Web site privacy policy," meaning a subset of the company's overall privacy policy, that may be acceptable, but the exact wording can be critical.

Company-wide implications: The FTC considers privacy policies posted on a company's Web site to be equally applicable to the company's off-line data collection, use, and disclosure practices—unless the company clearly states that the Web site privacy policy applies only to its online activities. In other words, what you say on your Web site has serious implications for data handling throughout the rest of the company.

The need to put up a privacy statement on the Web site actually introduced many companies to privacy as an issue. This was partly because a lot of companies had not previously thought of privacy as something about which it was necessary to have a policy, and also because a lot of today's companies are no older than their Web sites. Quite naturally, in many of these companies the Web site privacy statement has become the de facto privacy policy for the company. However, this can lead to problems because many companies now need—for both business and regulatory reasons—policies covering aspects of privacy that go beyond the Web.

Practical Steps

If you need a Web site privacy statement and want to get started right away there are places on the Web that you can go to for help. Several are described here, along with some serious caveats for those who might be tempted to take too many shortcuts.

The Better Business Bureau Online

The Better Business Bureau Online has a privacy seal program and provides a sample "Privacy Notice" at their web site (check the Sources section at www.privacyforbusiness.com or at the back of this book for the exact address of this and other pages mentioned here).

TRUSTe

You will also find a model privacy statement page at the TRUSTe Web site. TRUSTe is the non-profit organization behind the most widely recognized Web site trust seal. The TRUSTe model privacy statement is a good starting point, particularly if you later decide to obtain a Web trust seal for your site (as described in Chapter 9). This is more than simply a fill-in-the-blanks statement template. You are prompted to consider many of the important questions that must be answered for a privacy statement to be both appropriate and effective. Before you rush off to cut-and-paste your own version, your attention is drawn to five excellent pieces of advice on the TRUSTe model statement page:

1. Say what you do; Do what you say—The Golden Rule in privacy statements is "Do Not Lie." The only thing worse than not posting a privacy statement is to fraudulently claim a certain business practice. State and Federal governments do not look kindly on companies that claim one set of practices and follow another.

2. Tailor the Model Privacy Statement—The model statement will provide you with resources to begin developing your own privacy statement but you should be sure not to simply cut and paste. Use it as a starting point to create a statement tailored to your specific practices.

3. Privacy Statements are not Disclaimers—The communication of your company's privacy practices should express what is actually happening on the site, not what may happen, has happened or is planned for the future. In some cases, informing your users of the information gathering your company's site *does not* practice may be more effective.

4. Revisit your privacy statement frequently—A privacy statement is a living document, designed to clearly communicate your company's privacy practices, which, for many companies, change over time. Make sure you revisit your posted privacy statement to make sure it truly reflects your current practices.

5. Communicate your privacy practices to your entire company— In order to avoid information spills it is important to make sure that your entire company is aware of the policies within your privacy statement.

Adapting a model privacy statement to post on your Web site is not a quick fix for privacy problems. A privacy statement will make your site appear more sensitive to privacy but, as TRUSTe points out, the statement has to accurately reflect your actual practices or you could be accused of, and fined for, deceptive business practices.

The Direct Marketing Association

In the current privacy landscape you may well find The Direct Marketing Association portrayed as the bad guy. That is because the DMA, a trade association of which many of America's largest companies are members, has opposed privacy legislation that privacy advocates have advocated. And that's because, in matters affecting the ability of companies to engage in direct marketing, a practice engaged in by just about every brand name company you can name, and hundreds of thousands of smaller ones you can't, the DMA would prefer industry self-regulation to legislation.

One result of this has been a series of pro-privacy efforts on the part of the DMA to help companies self-regulate. That is why the DMA offers a free interactive Privacy Policy Generator on its Web site. After it has asked you questions about your web site the Privacy Policy Generator emails you a customized policy statement that reflects your responses. There are more than a dozen questions about web site practices that directly or potentially impact privacy. You might want to review the questions even if you do not submit your answers—it will help you assess the scope of the task ahead.

The OECD

The Organization for Economic Cooperation and Development (OECD) also offers a free privacy statement generator. Like the DMA generator, the OECD generator uses a question and answer approach. The result is a statement that references the OECD privacy guidelines (discussed in detail in Chapter 3).

IAPO

The International Association of Privacy Officers (IAPO) came into being when two organizations joined forces: the Privacy Officers Association (POA), and the Association of Corporate Privacy Officers (ACPO). The IAPO describes itself as "a unified voice for privacy professionals everywhere," and it is widely considered to be the leading professional organization for those people whose job it is to manage privacy for companies. The IAPO's charter is: "to work to promote, support, and enhance the skills and proficiency of privacy officers and other related professionals." As part of this work, IAPO has a Web site, and of course a privacy notice. This one is a good model for professional membership organizations and other entities that are not companies.

Practical Issues

Now you've had an opportunity to see what a privacy statement covers, it's time to think about what posting such a statement requires. One requirement is a review by the company lawyer. Unless he or she is well-versed in privacy, you may need to provide some background on what the privacy statement is intended to do, and where it fits in the company's overall privacy strategy (you could do worse than lend them a copy of this book). If the company does not have an overall privacy strategy then this section, as well as the following chapter, can help with that too.

For many companies the most demanding requirement, the biggest obstacle to putting up a defensible privacy statement, is the very practical one of determining what personal data the company is collecting, and what is being done with it. It is not unusual for a company to have developed numerous Web sites without having a definitive accounting as to the exact type of data processed. The answer is to map data flows.

Privacy Volunteers: A few years ago, it was typical for employees who were concerned about Web site security to be the ones who pushed the company to document its Web and network infrastructure. Today, employees concerned about privacy are often called upon to document the sources and uses of data that are handled by the company Web sites. There will be more detailed discussion of privacy roles and responsibilities in the next chapter, but for now, just bear in mind that speaking up about the need for a privacy statement could "volunteer" you for a lot of work.

Mapping Data Flows

Many companies find that when they try to get a handle on privacy, no definitive documentation is available as to what data is being collected, how or about whom it is being collected, or where it is being stored or sent. The person running the Web site can hardly be expected to answer these questions for the company as a whole, but he or she can be expected to answer them with respect to the Web site. Those answers will shape the part of the privacy statement that notifies users of the site, as to the type of data collected plus any "downstream" implications, such as a data-sharing agreement or cross-marketing with another organization.

The best way to tackle this is to track exactly what happens to PII from the moment it enters the system, for example when it is entered in a form on a Web page. Some forms on Web sites simply email the user input to a company email address when the "submit" button is clicked. A more sophisticated approach is to write the input to a file. The secure way to do this is to make sure the file is not stored on the Web server for any length of time, but spooled to a properly fire-walled back-end server. Access to data on that back-end server should be tightly restricted to employees who need to see it in order to perform their work. The access controls needed to do this are available in programs like Microsoft SQL Server, IBM DB2, Oracle and Sybase. However, database developers do not always implement them, sometimes because the company did not request them in the design specification.

The more complex and interactive the Web sites with which you are working, the more work it will take to create a complete data flow map. In practical terms, you might try using a large whiteboard for the project. A large plot of the appropriate network diagram(s) can also be a good starting point to which notes and references can be added. Here are the main points that need to be documented:

- Identification of the entity collecting the data.

- Identification of the intended use of the data.

- Identification of any potential recipients of the data.

- The nature of the data collected and the means by which it is collected, if not obvious (for example, passively, by means of electronic monitoring, or actively, by asking the consumer to provide the information).

- Whether the provision of the requested data is voluntary or required, and the consequences of a refusal to provide the requested information.

- The steps that the data collector has taken to ensure the confidentiality, integrity, and quality of the data.

The Interrogative Approach

Tracking down the facts about PII in your company may require above average investigative skills. A few observations based on past experience may help. There are two different and quite distinct approaches to finding where data live and who has access to them: interrogative and forensic. The interrogative approach involves asking the people who administer the systems that process the data. The amount of effort required by this approach varies considerably, depending on the size of the organization and the level of cooperation you receive—being tasked directly by the CPO or someone else at the CxO level can help with the latter. You could be looking at anything from a few informal discussions to a whole string of formal meetings.

The best approach is to pick a starting point and follow where it leads. If possible, start with someone that you know, someone with whom you enjoy a good working relationship. Ask them what they know. If they don't have all the answers, ask them for their recommendations, for example, to whom do they think you should talk. Ask for any documentation of the system that is available. Start creating your own version based on what you are being told. Use this to ask more detailed questions. Try a line that goes something like this: "Sorry to bother you Jim. I know you're busy, but the CxO has asked me to document all the uses we make of PII. I've started to draw this map of data flows in our system and I wonder if you have a minute to look it over and see if I'm getting it right."

Tact and Diplomacy: The interrogative approach works best if you have good people skills. If tact and diplomacy are not your strong suits, consider partnering with someone else who can do the talking. My colleagues and I have found this approach to be very effective, particularly in large organizations where people can be very territorial about "their" systems.

Try to stay focused and not become distracted. Remember that the end result you are looking for is a clear picture of how data gets into the system, where it resides, where it goes, and who gets to see it at each of those stages. In addition, you want an accompanying record of who "owns" the data at the various stages of its flow through the company, and how to contact them.

The Forensic Approach

Bear in mind that the results you get from the interrogative approach are dependent upon the accuracy of the responses to your questions. That is why you might want to try the forensic approach as well. The forensic approach looks for the answers from the systems themselves. Two things are required: tools and permission to use them. The tools are basically search programs that can look at the contents of files.

Of course, if all you wanted to do was look within a specific file you could use the application that created the file to perform the search (for example, querying a database). However, if you don't know which file or file type the target data is in, then a "low level" search is needed, wherein all files of every type are examined to see if they contain a certain string of characters that represents the target.

For example, if the target is credit card information, then you might ask the search tool to look for "5466 and VISA." The digits are a common credit card prefix number and any files that are found to contain it should be examined more closely to see if they contain actual credit card records. Other search terms might include combinations of area code prefixes, ZIP codes, and common last names.

Rather than get distracted by the technical details of how a forensic search works, a section on this topic has been placed on the Sources section of the www.privacyforbusiness.com site. Suffice to say that tools for forensic searches are available for both Windows and UNIX systems, and some are capable of searching across networks as well as through individual hard drives. Since the same tools are used by law enforcement agencies seeking evidence in criminal cases, and intelligence agencies trying to track classified data leaks, they should be employed with some sensitivity. However, they are definitely an option to consider.

Another forensic technique is to "seed" the company databases with a data "plant." In other words, go to the Web site, enter some data, and then use forensic tools to see where it shows up. You should do this from outside the company network, for example using a separate ISP account on a dial-up connection. Before you go to the company Web site, make a note of your IP address. That is one more identifier that you can look for within the company databases. Since a unique email address can be set up at no charge and in practically no time at all, using a service such as MSN Hotmail or Yahoo! Mail, this is one of the easiest ways to seed a database.

In fact, TRUSTe uses this technique as part of its oversight of privacy practices at companies that license its privacy seal. If the test address, which is used just once, at the target company's Web site, starts to receive email that falls outside the notice provided at the point where the address was submitted, then a flag is raised.

Web Specific Issues

The person responsible for the Web site may be asked to do some of the data mapping work, notably documenting Web specific issues like logging activity, the use of cookies, and the mapping of data flows. These will have practical implications for the privacy statement that eventually emerges. The following sections briefly discuss some of these issues, along with pointers on how they can be addressed when the statement is being written.

Logging Activity

You need to let visitors to your site know if you use automated tools to log information about their visits. Many sites use language along these lines:

> "We process information about visitors to our Web site in the aggregate to determine site performance issues, such as most popular pages, most frequently downloaded forms, and other site performance characteristics. This information does not identify you personally. We do not track or record information about individuals and their visits. This aggregated log data is processed by a software tool. The raw log data is retained for three months and is then destroyed."

To be completely clear and open about things, you might want to state specific data you collect, such as the following:

1. The Internet domain (for example, www.earthlink.net) and the Internet protocol (IP) address (the number that is assigned to your computer when you are surfing the Web).

2. The type of browser and operating system used to access our site.

3. The date and time you access our site.

4. The pages that are viewed, and paths that are taken through the Web site.

Use of Web Bugs and Beacons

If your Web site uses Web bugs or your email uses Web beacons, this should be disclosed, along with a clear statement of how and why they are used, and what information they track. Past "abuse" of this technology, plus some overly alarmist reporting, has made some consumers very sensitive to it, particularly when it is used to send data to a third party (for more on this topic, see the Sources section at the end of the book—or check out bugnosis.org, which covers the subject in great detail).

Use of Cookies

If your Web site uses cookies to enhance and improve visitor experience, this should be stated. A distinction should be made between *session* cookies, which expire when the user closes the Web browser, and *persistent* cookies, which are downloaded to the user's machine for future use on the site. You need to document, and may want to disclose, either in the site privacy statement or on specific pages that use them, what information is being collected by persistent cookies, why it is being collected, and how it is being used.

From Data to Policy and Back

At this point you should have a clearer picture of the information you need to write an appropriate Web site privacy statement and the resources that are available to help you complete the task. Once the statement has been written you will need to incorporate it into a broader company privacy policy. Of course, you might think that this chapter has the steps backwards. Here is the order so far:

- the need to post a Web site privacy statement,

- the tools to help you write the statement,

- the process of discovering the data you will need to complete the statement, and

- the need for detailed internal privacy policy documentation.

I realize it is possible to work the problem in the opposite direction, from the need for detailed internal privacy policy documentation to the need to post a Web site privacy statement. But the way this chapter has approached things reflects the natural progression—and the current reality—of the privacy issue at many companies.

Very few companies today can afford to sit down and start from scratch with privacy policy, and for those that can, the logical progression is obvious. You start with a general, high-level statement of company privacy policy and extrapolate from there to each area of business activity, getting more and more specific as you drill down to actual company practices and procedures. You create an internal document that guides employees and managers and a public statement that goes on the Web site and into customer mailings.

In the past, in the context of information security policy, I have been a big advocate of the "top-down" approach. But privacy is decidedly different from security. Furthermore, the business climate today is very different from a few years ago. Regardless of the degree to which privacy matters to you personally, the practical business reality is that privacy is only one of many pressing issues competing for corporate attention and budget dollars.

When, taking the high road of top-down policy development is not an option, you need a middle way (I will assume that you have ruled out the low road—doing nothing about privacy). A company's handling of privacy issues can evolve over time to cover all the bases. Starting at the point of greatest exposure, which for many companies is the Web site, is a logical and practical solution. Furthermore, until you have a clear idea of what PII the company currently handles and how, starting at the top can be risky—you don't want to end up with a policy that is at odds with practices on which the company relies for operations.

High-Level Policy

At the highest level, your company's privacy policy can be as short as a single sentence and should not be more than 50 words at the most. What you are aiming for is something that sums up the company's attitude to privacy in words that the CEO is prepared to recite publicly and sign personally. Consider these four examples:

Respect for customer privacy has always been a priority at Your Company.

Your Company respects the privacy of customers and maintains strict customer information privacy policies.

Your Company is committed to meeting customer expectations regarding the collection, control, use, transfer, storage and disclosure of personally identifiable information.

At Your Company, privacy means giving customers control over the collection, use, and distribution of their personal information in order to build and maintain trust and loyalty.

All of these work as a high-level statement than can be issued both publicly and internally. When issued publicly, for example in the Web site privacy statement, they constitute, or form part of, the preamble. When issued internally, they preface more detailed statements about the privacy responsibilities of managers and employees.

The way you phrase your high-level policy will depend on the type of business you are in. You might try wording it as though you were addressing a meeting of your shareholders, or just an individual customer. I am not exaggerating when I say you want to use "words that the CEO is prepared to recite publicly and sign personally." At least one company has taken this approach literally. Click on the Privacy link on FleetBoston Financial's home page and you are presented with a letter about privacy policy from the CEO.

Personally, I think this is quite impressive, particularly as the language used is very clear and direct. There is no wiggle room or sense of holding back when a company says: "We know how important your privacy is to you. And, at FleetBoston Financial, we're committed to protecting it." The CEO then removes any lingering doubts a customer might have about that commitment by publicly endorsing his company's privacy policy with his signature:

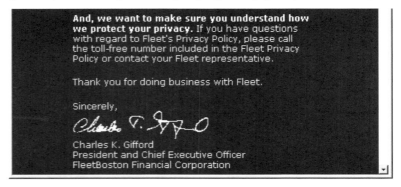

While this approach may not fit every business model or culture, when I tried some informal consumer research on this particular example, the reactions were very favorable. Here's a typical comment: "It tells me their privacy policy is not just there to meet regulations, it is something the CEO actually got involved with, otherwise he wouldn't be putting his name to it so publicly."

Internal v. External

One notable way in which privacy differs from security in the area of policy is that companies are expected to provide a public statement of their privacy policy, at least with respect to certain aspects of the business, such as the Web site. Companies have not been in the habit of publishing security policy statements. We are now seeing some very general security statements accompanying privacy statements, such as this one from FleetBoston Financial:

> "The security of your information is a priority to us. We maintain physical, electronic, and procedural safeguards that comply with federal standards to protect customer information."

Nevertheless, security policy is typically thought of as an internal matter, and security policy documents can get pretty specific about how information is to be protected. Security policies are not something a company will want to make public; but privacy policy has entered the corporate and consumer consciousness via the very public Web, and thus tends to be thought of as something you make public.

In fact, your company should put together separate privacy documentation that is for internal use only, and do so just as soon as it can. Until you have such documentation, and until it has been read by those that need to read it, you will have a hard time keeping the promises you make in your public privacy statements, and an even harder time defending your company's track record on privacy should any of those promises be broken.

From Policies Down to Procedures

Once the high-level privacy policy has been agreed, you can use it as the starting point for privacy policies in different areas of the business. These can then be embodied in company procedures. Here is a good example, from AT&T, of how to take the first step. Consider this high-level statement:

> "AT&T has a long-standing tradition of recognizing and protecting the privacy of customers who use its telecommunications networks. The company maintains strict customer information privacy policies and uses state of the art technologies to safeguard customer information and communications from unauthorized intrusions."

From General to Online

The preceding works for all aspects of the company's operations, as both an internal and an external statement. Now look at the natural extrapolation to address online services:

> "AT&T recognizes that the growth of online services, including Internet services, has created additional privacy concerns, particularly for consumers. Online privacy concerns focus primarily on the protection of "customer identifiable" information which an individual or other customer reasonably expects to be kept private."

These are in fact the first two paragraphs of AT&T's statement of its online privacy policy on the main company Web site. You will find the same high-level policy at the Web sites of different AT&T divisions. And perhaps it is not surprising that similar wording is used by other companies, with company specific adjustments. Here are some examples, with the actual company names removed:

> "XYZ has a long-standing tradition of recognizing and protecting the privacy of customers who use its billing and customer care solutions."

> "Protecting the privacy of our customers and clients is an absolute 'must' at PQR. We have a long-standing tradition of recognizing and protecting the privacy of customers who utilize our services and purchase products from our firm."

While the above are published statements of high-level privacy policy they work just as well as the starting point of internal policy documentation. Both hint at the next level of detail that is needed. For example, XYZ will need to address privacy issues specific to users of the company's billing solutions, as well as to users of its customer care solutions.

From External to Internal

How your company extrapolates privacy policy internally will depend upon company structure. For example, if your company is very vertically structured into business divisions based on product lines, then each division may need its own privacy policies, particularly if the different divisions have different markets, such as consumer and commercial, domestic and foreign. If the company is divided into function-based groups—such as accounting, marketing, HR, and production—then privacy policies for each will be needed. This includes aspects of privacy unrelated to the Web, like employee privacy, that are not addressed here (see the Sources section at www.privacyforbusiness.com for more on this topic).

As the company creates its internal privacy documentation, one of the key challenges will be ensuring company-wide compliance with the privacy commitments that the company has made to the public. This extends well beyond the Web and email. For example, who does the privacy review when the marketing department wants to include a sweepstakes entry form in the bills your company mails to its customers, in order to collect names and addresses for future customer acquisition mailings? If your particular interest is the Web site you will want to watch this type of thing very closely. For example, the marketing department could just as easily decide to run a sweepstakes competition on the Web site. Fortunately, most companies today have some form of Web content management system in place that requires new Web projects such as this to be reviewed, but not necessarily from a privacy perspective.

From Content Management to Privacy

Content management normally arises from technical and logistical issues. However, the controls it puts in place can be expanded to include privacy. Thus you might have an internal privacy policy that states:

> "All new Web projects involving the collection, use, or sharing of PII must comply with company privacy policy."

The associated procedure might state that:

> "All new Web projects involving the collection, use, or sharing of PII must be reviewed by X."

Obviously, X represents the appropriate person, committee, or other entity within your organization, such as the content management committee. I used X because a standard way of handling this within companies has yet to emerge, and because it brings us to the next order of business, privacy strategy.

Privacy Strategy

There will be a lot more about this subject in the next chapter but I wanted to introduce it here because the privacy policies I have been talking about in this chapter will prove difficult to implement unless you have a privacy strategy. In this sense, privacy strategy completes the "reverse" order of business that this chapter has followed. In an ideal world you would start with strategy, deciding how the company wanted to approach the issue and who would play what role. You might decide that the best place to start would be the creation of a chief privacy officer position, or the forming of an executive committee on privacy. Such an entity could then craft the high-level privacy policy and guide its extrapolation into company-wide privacy policies and procedures.

Companies that have the luxury of starting fresh and doing things right will know the right way to go (as diagrammed in Figure 6-1). But most companies are already in the privacy trenches, looking for a chance to regroup. They are forming privacy strategy even as they publish privacy statements and draft privacy procedures. The ones that are successful will be able to leverage privacy as a brand-enhancing market differentiator, minimizing the risk of privacy incidents while sticking to their business plan.

Figure 6-1: Privacy policy development plan.

CHAPTER SEVEN

STRATEGY AND INCIDENT RESPONSE

010101101110011011111010010111001010101011011011

"Plans and procedures must be created to ensure effective response to, and mitigation of damage from, whatever privacy incidents occur in spite of your good faith prevention efforts. The message is: Prevent what you can. Prepare for what you can't."

—Vincent Schiavone, President and CEO, ePrivacy Group.

7: Strategy and Incident Response

Putting together a corporate privacy policy requires a large amount of corporate decision-making, which in turn requires a corporate strategy with respect to privacy. Such a strategy must include more than what you say about privacy; it must cover what you do, including what you do when things go wrong. The goal of this chapter is to help you develop your company's privacy strategy and privacy incident preparedness. I begin with a privacy scenario, the purpose of which is to establish some common ground, a set of circumstances that will serve as a basis for discussing several different aspects of privacy strategy and response to privacy incidents, even if you have been fortunate enough, so far, to avoid any such incidents.

A Typical Privacy Scenario

This incident begins when a fax arrives at Your Company headquarters, addressed to the CEO. The irate sender of the fax says that a company that got her email address from yourcompany.com has spammed her. She alleges that Your Company sold her email address to a third party without her permission, a violation of the privacy statement at yourcompany.com. She is vowing never to patronize Your Company again and hinting that she will file complaints with the Federal Trade Commission, EPIC, MAPS Realtime Blackhole List, the Attorney General of the state in which she lives, and anyone else she can think of. The CEO is perturbed. She calls a meeting. Because you have overall responsibility for the Web site at yourcompany.com, you are invited. What do you do?

Reality Check

The first step is to make sure you know what this person is talking about, just in case the CEO asks for an explanation. If you have read the chapters leading up to this one you know what the FTC is, and that it has an interest in consumer complaints about privacy and spam. While this particular complaint does not appear to have the scope or gravity of the Prozac Email Incident or the Passport False Promises Case, you are aware that the FTC is quite capable of taking on the richest, most powerful companies in the world and imposing costly settlements on them in matters of privacy, security, and the Internet.

The fax that the CEO received also mentions EPIC and you may have noted from previous chapters that EPIC is the Electronic Privacy Information Center. This non-profit advocacy group is notable in this context as one of the organizations that persuaded the FTC to take on Microsoft over privacy and security issues surrounding its Passport service.

The mention of MAPS might throw you at first, unless you happen to be responsible for your company's email system, in which case you may know of MAPS already. Short for Mail Abuse Prevention System, MAPS is a non-profit organization, the goal of which is "to defend the Internet's email system from abuse by spammers." MAPS seek to do this "by educating and encouraging ISP's to enforce strong terms and conditions prohibiting their customers from engaging in abusive email practices." To this end, MAPS operates the Real Time Black Hole List (RBL). There will be more about spam and black holes in the next chapter, but for now it is enough to know that you do not want to find your company on the RBL, because that will prevent your company's email from getting delivered (an increasing number of Internet Service Providers are refusing to deliver email that comes from addresses that are on the RBL).

Mapping Email: MAPS^{SM} is a service mark of Mail Abuse Prevention System, LLC, as is RBL^{SM}. The term "black hole list" is more generic but my personal preference is to use the term "block list."

Now that you have the acronyms covered, the next item in your reality check, ahead of your close encounter with the CEO, is an initial determination as to the claim that Your Company sold someone's email address to a third party, without permission, and in violation of the privacy statement on the company Web site. You are aware of only two places on the Web site where visitors can input email addresses. One is a form for requesting assistance on the technical support page; the other is a form for requesting product news and information. A call to the Webmaster confirms that this is still the case. You print out a copy of the Web site privacy statement and head to the meeting.

The Incident Meeting

When the meeting convenes, the CEO and corporate counsel are in attendance, joined by yourself and the heads of customer service, marketing, and technical support. The CEO hands out copies of the complaint and asks all of you to report. The company lawyer states that legal action is unlikely because the offended party has suffered very little in the way of damages and this appears to be an isolated incident. The EPIC/FTC/MAPS threat is not significant because Your Company is not doing the spamming and it would be hard to prove Your Company sold the address to another company.

The manager of technical support states that his department is not aware of anyone copying data from customer records to use for marketing and, as far as he can tell, the woman who complained is not in their database. Customer service says the same. The head of marketing states that the names and email addresses of people who sign up to get product news are not sold or rented out. Furthermore, he says the page where people sign up clearly states "you are giving us your email address so that we can send you information of the stated type." Finally, he notes that the Web site's privacy statement assures people their PII will not be shared and as far as he is aware, it is not.

Now it's your turn. You confirm what marketing has said about the forms on the Web site and the privacy statement. You note that the irate fax uses the term "sold" with reference to the third party obtaining the woman's address, and it would be helpful to ask her why she thought that, however, she did not include her phone number. You also point out that the fax contains a copy of the email message that the woman received, but without all of the headers, which could be useful in tracking down the problem. The CEO asks what headers are, which gives you an opportunity to impress. You explain that they are the part of an email message that describes the originator, the addressee and other recipients, message priority level, and so on. Often this information is masked by the email program, but can be revealed if you use the appropriate command (check out Chapter 8 for more detail on email headers).

The CEO asks for suggestions. Legal suggests the company ignore the matter. Customer service suggests sending a fax to the woman who complained, providing three things:

1. an apology for any inconvenience caused by the unwanted email,

2. an assurance that selling of names is against Your Company policy,

3. a promise to investigate further (while noting that at this time there appears to be no evidence that anyone at Your Company supplied her name to another company).

Legal objects that this is too close to an admitting that there is a problem but the CEO feels it is important to be responsive, especially since the woman indicated she had patronized the company in the past. You suggest that someone be tasked with searching the company network for any mention of this woman. If there is none, and if no more complaints are received within the next 24 hours, then the company can be more confident in the wording of its response. The CEO agrees, and tasks you with the search.

Privacy Investigator

As any successful shopkeeper will tell you, communication is the key to handling customer complaints. You have to listen well and ask the right questions. Sometimes it is not possible, as in this case, to ask the person directly. But you can make some assumptions based on your reading of the customer's statement, and then ask yourself some questions. In this case, the woman seems quite certain of two things: a. Your Company got her name from the Web site, b. Your Company sold her name to the company that spammed her. So, where would she get an idea like that? Discounting the possibility that she dreamed it up or jumped to conclusions, you should at least try to answer this question.

Customer Conversations: One of the challenges of doing business electronically is that you are seldom in conversation with the customer. Unlike a phone conversation, in which both parties can respond to each other in real time, fax and email exchanges are asynchronous, meaning one direction at a time. A phone call handled by a trained customer service professional can often placate an irate customer more quickly and effectively than a series of emails or other correspondence. If you don't have permission to call the customer, the phone call may not be seen as an option, but there is nothing to stop the customer service department using an email or fax to ask the customer for permission to call them to resolve the matter.

One place to look for answers would be the company that allegedly spammed this person, except such companies can be hard to find, particularly without a full set of headers. Another tack is the one you suggested in the meeting: rule out the possibility that her name was sold because Your Company never had her name. If your company has already been through the process of mapping data flows, as described in Chapter 6, this should be a relatively easy task to accomplish.

Mapping data flows is a way to track what happens to PII from the moment it enters the system, for example when it is entered in a form on a Web page. The end result you are looking for in this scenario is a clear picture of how data gets into the system, where it resides, where it goes, and who gets to see it at each of those stages. Then you will know where to look for the target data, the irate customer's email address that was allegedly shared with another company in violation of privacy policy. You will also know who had an opportunity to violate the privacy policy. However, bear in mind that abuse of authorized access, such as the marketing manager burning a CD of the customer database and selling it to another company, is only one of many ways that data can leak. You must also consider the possibility that someone may gain unauthorized access to data.

As discussed in Chapter 6, there are two different and quite distinct approaches to finding where data lives and who has access to it: interrogative and forensic. The interrogative approach proceeds by asking the people who administer the systems that process the data. The results that you get from the interrogative approach depend upon the accuracy of the responses to your questions. That is why you might want to try the forensic approach as well, or instead.

The forensic approach looks for the answers from the systems themselves. Two things are required: tools and permission to use them. The tools are basically search programs that can look at the contents of files. Of course, if all you wanted to do was look within a specific file you could use the application that created the file to perform the search (for example, querying a database). However, if you don't know which file or file type the target data is in, then a "low level" search is needed, wherein all files of every type are examined to see if they contain a particular string of characters that represents the target.

For example, if the target is Jane Doe whose email address is jane4ever@aol.com, then you would want the search tool to look for the string: jane4ever@aol.com. This will result in fewer false positives than searching for Jane Doe, since email addresses are unique. There is more about forensic searches in the Sources section at www.privacyforbusiness.com. Tools for forensic searches are available for both Windows and Unix systems. Some are capable of searching across networks as well as through local hard drives.

Since the same tools are used by law enforcement agencies seeking evidence in criminal cases, and intelligence agencies trying to track classified data leaks, they should be employed with some sensitivity. You do not want your fellow employees to misconstrue what you are doing. However, such tools are definitely an option to consider, particularly if the results of the interrogative approach are inconclusive.

Problem Solving

Let us assume that you have asked your questions and performed your searches. What are some of the possible findings and responses, given the original scenario of a customer complaining that Your Company sold her email address?

No Trace

You uncover no evidence that the woman who complained was ever in your system. If you are confident that this is the case, then the company's response might read something like this:

Dear Ms. Doe,

Customer privacy is very important to us at Your Company. Because our privacy policy forbids the sale or unauthorized sharing of customer information, your fax concerns us deeply. However, a careful examination of our systems found no sign that the email address at which you received the offending spam message was ever in our records. We would like to help you more but this will require additional information that was not in the fax you sent. May we have your permission to call you, at a convenient time and number, to discuss this matter further?

Sincerely,

Your Company

You don't want to say, "we think you made a mistake." But that may well be what happened. Many companies have experienced complaints about "spam" from people who have forgotten that they asked to receive the information they are now calling spam. Few consumers keep track of where or to whom they have provided their email address.

Of course, there is another explanation, the plausibility of which depends upon several factors, including the strength of your network security. Is it possible that the customer's name and email address was on the system but someone copied it, sold it, and then deleted it?

If the company has only received one complaint, and there are no other indications, such as marketing complaining that the Web site is not generating enough leads, then speculation about theft of data might be considered paranoid. However, there is no doubt that thefts of this type do occur, although deleting the data after copying is probably less common than just copying and leaving the original in place.

Trace Evidence

If the customer's information is found in one of the company databases then the situation is quite different. The data flows you have mapped will be needed to determine how plausible it is that the information was passed to another company. Unless someone owns up to doing a deal that is against company policy, further detective work may be required. Here are some possibilities to consider:

An employee sold the data: you have a serious problem that should be dealt with at the highest level. The customer has a legitimate complaint and there may be many others like her. Attempt to determine exactly what data were sold. Contact the purchaser and request a halt to use of the data. Consider pre-emptive contact with affected persons and inform them that, due to an employee's violation of company policy, their name may have been shared with another company. Apologize and explain steps taken to rectify.

An outsider obtained and sold the data: this indicates a serious security problem and should be handled at the highest level. You may want to contact law enforcement. Although the customer's accusation that the company willfully sold her data is incorrect, the company has failed in its duty to protect that information and could face state or federal investigation. Attempt to determine exactly what data were sold. Contact the purchaser and request a halt to use of the data. Consider pre-emptive contact with affected persons as in the previous outcome.

An employee shared the data: this is a violation of policy with potentially damaging consequences. The fact that the data were shared rather than sold may allow the company to put a different spin on the incident, which can be characterized as "misguided employee violates policy." You remove the impression of greed that surrounds the selling of the data, but you still need to determine exactly what data were shared and ask the other company to stop using it. Consider pre-emptive contact with affected persons as in the previous outcome.

Nobody sold or shared the data: this is possible because the customer could be wrong. The other company could have got her email address from somewhere else. However, an effort should be made to get more information from the customer, namely a detailed explanation of why she thinks her name was sold.

Lessons Learned

Now it is time to step back and look at this whole process and see what can be learned. In fact, this is a golden rule common to all forms of incident management: learn whatever you can from the incident. This will help you prevent further incidents and perform better if/when another one occurs.

The first lesson is that the company needs to know, at any given time, and in considerable detail, what data its Web site is handling, what exactly happens to that data, and who has access to it. That knowledge will enable the company to respond rapidly and confidently to potential incidents. Furthermore, the gathering of that knowledge may reveal and forestall potential privacy incidents.

The second lesson is that simply having a privacy policy is not enough; the policy has to be enforced. That means all employees affected by the policy must know what it is and know that violations will have consequences. If violations are routinely ignored, it may become impossible to discipline violators, thus rendering the policy ineffectual (the courts found, for example, that when someone was fired for not protecting her network password, the dismissal was in fact unfair because management was aware that passwords were often left unprotected and did nothing about it).

The third lesson is that a privacy incident can consume a lot of time and distract a lot of people. Chapter 2 illustrated the costs of privacy incidents with some estimates produced by Forester Research. These were broken down into the following categories:

- CEO/president time
- Management time
- PR Meetings and calls
- Management press calls
- Management review of privacy practices
- Customer service calls and emails

- Employee communications and training

- External consultants

- Travel

Some of the outcomes in our very simple scenario could conceivably incur costs in all of these categories. If the customer list really was sold by someone who had hacked into the company network, then the company could face civil suits, state and federal investigations, and press coverage. Damage control would be required, at the public and the customer level, as well as remediation through employee education.

The fourth lesson is that steps should be taken to prevent a recurrence. This encompasses more than lesson two, the enforcement of privacy policies. The company should look at data handling procedures and data security measures to see where improvements can be made to prevent similar problems in the future.

Privacy training for managers and employees should be stepped up, not only because privacy-aware employees are your best hope of heading off potential privacy incidents, but also because a privacy-training program is a good defense should further incidents occur. If the company can show that employees were trained to know better, the company and its management may be exonerated.

The fifth lesson is that dealing with privacy requires both leadership and a group effort. Privacy problems cut across all aspects of company operations, from IT to marketing, legal to PR, operations to upper management.

Anyone appointed to deal with a privacy problem will not only need access to these areas and a solid understanding of how they work, but also a good dose of confidence and plenty of people skills. Furthermore, in a company of any size, the appointed person will also need support, some sort of committee, group, or team.

Blue Collar Privacy: Although it is natural for a book about Web site and email privacy to focus on the protection of people's data while it is being processed or transmitted, you should not overlook the many non-computer forms that PII can take. For example, if the purpose of your Web site is to take orders for products that have to be physically delivered to customers, have you thought about the potential exposure and abuse of PII in the shipping department? Of necessity, the shipping department has to know the names and addresses of customers. If the company has thought about protecting that information from competitors there may be some data protection policies and procedures in place, but what about the privacy implications? Based on the actual products you ship, these may not be inconsiderable. On its own, a name and address is not necessarily sensitive, but place it on a package of anti-depressants or a catalog of sexually explicit videos, and it suddenly becomes very sensitive. Similar issues arise in mail room operations for things like medical invoices, and so on.

Enter the CPO

When companies get to grips with privacy they often find themselves asking, "Is privacy a legal matter or a compliance issue, a brand management function or a security matter?" The answer, as you have probably guessed, is "Yes, yes, yes, and yes." The privacy issues that companies face today involve aspects of legal, compliance, PR, marketing, business development, consumer relations, branding, and security.

In other words, privacy is inherently inter-departmental in function and heavily inter-disciplinary in terms of skill set. That sounds like a recipe for a committee—and management of privacy by committee will be discussed later in the chapter—however, committees are seldom a good way to handle responsibility or accountability.

As the privacy scenario illustrated, one of the biggest problems companies encounter when faced with their first privacy challenge is a lack of responsibility or accountability for privacy. While there may be some people within management who are more concerned and informed about privacy than others, what the company really needs is someone who is prepared to step up and say "I will take the lead on privacy for our company and you can hold me accountable for how well we do."

That is precisely what a colleague of mine, Ray Everett-Church, did a number of years ago when he was working at an Internet company that faced public criticism of its business model from privacy advocates. In effect, Ray invented the role of Chief Privacy Officer, a position in keeping with the standard business practice of appointing chief officers for business functions where leadership and accountability are important, such as finance (CFO), information (CIO), technology (CTO), and, more recently, security (CSO).

Since then, the executive position of CPO has been rapidly adopted across corporate America (by the end of 2000 the position existed at the following companies and more: American Express, AT&T, IBM, General Motors. Microsoft, Sybase, Verizon, IBM). Despite isolated criticism from a few privacy advocates—who have dismissed CPOs as corporate window dressing—the CPO position has received broad support across the Internet community. My own experience working with a number of CPOs strongly suggests that when a company creates a CPO position at the executive level, it is taken seriously, by the company *and* the person who fills it.

One example of support in the advocate community is a group called Computer Professionals for Social Responsibility, which describes itself as "a public-interest alliance of computer scientists and others concerned about the impact of computer technology on society." Hardly a fan of corporate America, CPSR has supported the move to appoint CPOs. The CPSR Privacy Working Group went so far as to distribute a document called *The CPO Guidelines*, which does an excellent job of defining the role of the CPO. Here is how Keith P. Enright and Michael R. McCullough, the authors of *The CPO Guidelines*, describe the benefits of appointing a CPO:

> "a talented and properly-positioned CPO will add value across corporate divisions from development to customer relations, from liability mitigation and risk management to increased market share and valuation. Perhaps most importantly, the Chief Privacy Officer promotes an essential element of new economy corporate citizenship—Trust."

CPO Roles and Reporting

Providing a complete CPO manual is beyond the scope of this book. The purpose of this section is to outline the role that the CPO can play in a company's privacy strategy. Obviously, that role will vary from company to company, as will the position's reporting structure. The optimal situation, according to *The CPO Guidelines*, is for the CPO to report to "the chief executive officer, president, chief operating officer, or executive director, also providing such reports to the board of directors as may be required from time to time."

Given the reality of corporate politics, it is perhaps unrealistic to expect to find the optimal being achieved in a large percentage of cases, but there are plenty of high profile examples that show it is possible, even when company politics mean the official title of the CPO is not CPO.

The creation of the CPO position is particularly tricky in certain industries such as banking and health care. Businesses in these sectors are required to comply with a whole range of state and federal regulations in many areas besides privacy, and many have a Corporate Compliance Officer or CCO position. Some of these organizations feel it is natural to place compliance with privacy laws under the established CCO position. However, as I have argued in this book and elsewhere, privacy for businesses is about a lot more than compliance with privacy laws, important as such compliance is. Does this mean that compliance expands to include these roles? Does the CPO have enough to do in addition to privacy compliance?

Questions like these are being asked in many companies right now. Clearly, there are no definitive, one -size-fits-all answers. The simple fact is that many companies are finding the creation and integration of such a potentially far-reaching executive position as CPO to be a challenge, the scale of which becomes clear when you look more closely at the possible roles and responsibilities of the CPO. Here is a summary of the core objectives and responsibilities of the CPO according to *The CPO Guidelines*:

- Establish and promote a privacy philosophy across the whole enterprise.

- Audit and assess information flows across and between organizations, identifying and addressing privacy implications of such flows.

- Identify applicable state, local, and federal regulations and, from such inputs, establish appropriate policies and procedures.

- Define institutional privacy goals and objectives, ensure policies reflect goals and objectives; supervise.

- Promote essential privacy policy elements organization-wide, including: Notice, Choice, Access, Security, Recourse, and Verification.

- Identify critical data systems and sensitive data; cooperate with other executives to ensure proper security and adherence to information handling practices.

- Educate and train staff members regarding institutional privacy philosophy, policies and procedures.

- Remain vigilant against privacy-compromising events and situations.

- Continually assess progress.

Clearly, those who take on this role will have their hands full. I will offer some suggestions on how to handle the workload after I define the role in a little more detail.

Twin Roles

As Ray Everett-Church points out with considerable humor in his privacy officer training sessions, the CPO role is two-faced, by which he means that the CPO has both an internal and an external role, both of which are equally important. The internal role includes participation in such internal processes as:

- company-wide strategy planning.

- business development and contract review.

- product development and implementation.

- company operations.

- security and fraud activities, and

- employee training and awareness.

If this makes it sound like the CPO is going to poke his or her nose in just about every corner of the company, then you have the right idea, but not the right attitude. While no CPO should give the impression of "poking," no department or division should object to CPO "input" any more than they object to input from the CIO, the CFO, or the CSO.

The external role of the CPO involves enhancing the company's public image as well as fostering positive relationships with consumers and consumer groups, privacy advocates, industry peers, and regulators. The external role includes:

- industry relations.

- government relations.

- media and PR relations.

- consumer relations, and

- outreach and profile in the privacy community.

In other words, the CPO becomes the company's flag-bearer and point person on privacy. For larger companies that have decided to make their handling of privacy a market differentiator, the CPO's external role may take on "evangelist" dimensions, with speaking engagements at industry conferences, press interviews and government advocacy.

Since most companies would prefer privacy self-regulation to government privacy regulation, there may be a tendency for the CPO to be drawn, or pushed, into a lobbyist role. However, overt lobbying by the CPO should be avoided. While the CPO most definitely works for the company, the position is most effective if it is perceived as objective, with ombudsman-like qualities, protective customer and consumer interests as well as those of the company. Of course, the CPO can certainly play an important role informing the company's privacy lobbying efforts.

Another way of breaking down the CPO role is to look at the privacy implications of existing business and new business. The existing business side of things involves the assessment of current data flows and PII handling practices, as well as the privacy implications of current contracts and Web/email operations.

The new business side of the CPO role means involvement or, at a minimum, review of plans for new products and services, new business partnerships or alliances that require coordination of privacy policies, planned enhancements of databases such as augmentation, and any mergers or acquisitions where due diligence requires investigation of another company's privacy polices and the "cleanliness" of any PII that is valued in the deal.

Action Plan: Knowing, Saying, Doing

If there is a CPO creed or mantra it might go like this: Know what you do. Say what you do. Do what you say. This is how Ray Everett-Church has articulated the CPO action plan and I appreciate his permission to outline it here.

Know What You Do

You must understand the company's data gathering practices, at both the division level and department level. Be aware of business development deals and marketing plans—these can have a major impact on data acquisition and use. Understand what standard of "permission" the company is using—if no standard is being used, determine the different levels of permission that different departments have established with respect to their data. Be aware of "legacy" databases and past data practices. Assess the company's defensive measures with respect to both outsiders and insiders— firewalls, intrusion detection, and role-based access controls.

Say What You Do

At lot of this is accomplished by the drafting or revision of the company's privacy policy. Clearly disclose all relevant practices— notice, choice, access, security, and redress. Be prepared to either adjust company practices or the wording of policies to make sure they are consistent—try to balance accuracy and detail with broad language that provides flexibility. If a change of policy is required, make the changes loud and clear. State your case and let consumers make their choices.

Do What You Say

Get a Chief Privacy Officer and build a privacy team—designate privacy point persons in all departments, particularly business development, product management and development, operations, compliance, legal, and regulatory. Implement ongoing security and data audits. Integrate privacy into your corporate message, both internally (employee education) and externally (to consumers, industry associations, regulatory bodies). Once the company is on track and problem areas have been resolved, get certified through organizations such as TRUSTe and BBBOnline, to demonstrate privacy commitment and compliance (but remember that certification by itself is not a guarantee of compliance).

Tips and Turf Wars

In this section I have rounded up advice for CPOs on a variety of topics, beginning with strong encouragement to reach out and touch other CPOs. Participation with your peers in industry associations is the best way to stay on top of privacy news, trends, and new developments in all areas, but especially legal, legislative, and regulatory. I strongly urge you to join the International Association of Privacy Officers. You don't have to be a CPO to join, just someone who has, or takes, responsibility for privacy in your organization.

Build privacy policies and audit rights into agreements with business partners, suppliers, and associates. They may be your friends, and they may be vital to your business, but they represent a major privacy exposure if their privacy standards are lax. In an effort to head off "weakest link" exposure, companies that are taking the lead on privacy are increasing likely to demand that the companies with which they do business contractually commit to appropriate privacy standards.

Be prepared to answer a lot of questions. A number of CPOs have told me that this was their biggest surprise after being appointed, and their biggest burden. The CPO can quickly become the lightning rod for privacy issues that have been building up within the company. Here's an example: what are the privacy implications of the company sending letters to retirees encouraging them to lobby the government on an issue of concern to the company? This may not be the sort of question you expected to get when you stepped up for the CPO position, but be prepared for even weirder ones than that, as well as their internal repercussions.

Consider consulting outside experts. The larger consulting firms usually want you to commission a broad and very expensive "baseline" privacy audit, but this is seldom the best approach (for one thing, a baseline privacy audit can too easily end up as evidence used against you). Consider retaining experts to whom you can turn for smaller projects, like researching some of the tougher questions you get asked, or providing a second opinion, an objective sanity-check that is not clouded by internal politics. And if you have to deal with privacy problems overseas, engage local expertise and local legal counsel that knows the regulatory landscape.

Gird yourself for turf wars. If the question of who should be in charge of privacy has not been addressed in your company yet, it is probably just a matter of time, and it can easily lead to turf wars. You can probably expect some people to make the case that the CPO should be a lawyer. This can work, *if* the lawyer is prepared to be CPO first and lawyer second. The appointment of a CPO is a business strategy and the CPO needs to maintain a business perspective, which is not always the same as a legal perspective.

Consider what happens when you buy software for your computer. The bright shiny box on the store shelf tells you all the things that the software will do for you. This is the business perspective. When you get the software home, you find you can't even install it unless you accept the maker's disclaimer that it may not do anything for you at all. This is the legal perspective.

Mind Your Language: Software licenses these days often say things like "The Company provides to you the software 'as is' and with all faults" and "The Company hereby disclaims all warranties including fitness for a particular purpose, lack of viruses, accuracy or completeness, workmanlike effort and lack of negligence." As the user, you are advised that "the entire risk arising out of use or performance of the software remains with you...The Company shall not be liable for any damages including loss of profits, loss of confidential information, business interruption, loss of privacy, and any other loss whatsoever...even if The Company has been advised of the possibility of such damages.

Lawyers will argue that such disclaimers are forced on "The Company" by an excessively litigious society. Be that as it may, no software company is going to put this type of legalese front and center on its Web site and you don't want your Web site's privacy profile to be dictated by the legal requirements. Building your privacy positioning on legalese is not good business. A legal review of privacy policies and statements is very important, but so is building a relationship of trust and confidence with your customers.

The Privacy Team

By now it should be clear that the skill set required to successfully manage privacy is extremely broad. While the appointment of a CPO provides privacy leadership and accountability within the company, it by no means assures that all of the privacy work will get done—as noted earlier, it can even generate or expose many privacy issues that heretofore were not recognized or addressed. The answer may be a privacy team of some sort.

If the CPO has budget for support staff, they should be chosen based on their ability to add to the overall skill set. For example, if the CPO is not a lawyer, then legal expertise might be added through a support position. If the CPO is a lawyer, then support staff with operations knowledge might be a valuable addition to the team. Technical expertise, particularly important if the company has a strong Internet presence or is heavily involved in data processing, can be added in this way also.

Even without budget, a privacy team can be assembled. This can be formal or informal, a privacy committee or a privacy working group, whatever works within, and is appropriate to, your company culture. One creative approach I have seen is a privacy brown-bag lunch group at a company that has lots of different divisions under one CPO. The CPO organizes this twice a month. Employees who serve as privacy "point person" for their group attend and they are able to network with their counterparts in an informal atmosphere. Presentations by outside experts and relevant vendors are used to encourage attendance and raise knowledge and awareness levels.

Privacy team membership should include as many of the major areas of the business as possible. These include, although not necessarily in order of importance: IT, legal, marketing, business development, product development, operations, security (both computer security and business security), human resources, and internal training/communications.

As I mentioned earlier in this chapter, the creation of a new executive-level position at your company may well put some people on the defensive. Consequently, efforts by the new CPO to build a privacy team may be seen by some as "empire building." There are several ways to deflect such criticism. One way is to cultivate an informal network of sympathetic, privacy-aware individuals within the various parts of your organization.

Privacy Incident Response

Ready for some good news? If you have followed the advice given in the book so far, creating and implementing sound privacy policies backed by increased privacy awareness among employees, mid-level managers, and executives, then you will significantly increase your chances of avoiding a damaging Web-related privacy incident.

The bad news is, however much effort you put into your privacy program, the probability of such incidents occurring never reaches zero (for those who skipped statistics class, a probability of zero means there's no chance it will happen). The implication? Your company is not completely up to speed on privacy unless it is ready to respond to a privacy incident when it does occur. Getting ready to respond is what this section is about. You will learn what constitutes a privacy incident, what sort of impact a privacy incident can have, and how to put together a Privacy Incident Response Team.

The Privacy Incident Response Team

The idea of a Privacy Team was discussed earlier in the context of supporting the CPO. This same team may form the basis of the Privacy Incident Response Team (PIRT) but it is important to be clear that the role of the PIRT is not to manage privacy on a day-to-day basis. The PIRT has a specific and fairly narrow objective, to respond to privacy incidents when they happen. If you are familiar with computer security, then you will recognize the Response Team concept, developed to handle major security incidents. The role of the Computer Incident Response Team, or CIRT, is to spring into action when a computer-related emergency threatens the confidentiality, integrity, or availability of the company's computer-based information and/or information systems.

Many companies now have a CIRT, a group of people that typically includes management personnel with the authority to act, technical personnel with the skills needed to fix problems, and communications experts with the ability to report status in a positive manner. The role of a PIRT, or Privacy Incident Response Team, is akin to that of the CIRT, but tasked with responding to the sort of privacy incidents that have been described throughout this book.

There may be times when an incident calls for activation of both the CIRT and PIRT, for example, when there is a Web site break-in that exposes customer PII. But there are also incidents to which CIRT or PIRT would respond alone (for example, CIRT alone would respond to a Denial of Service attack that prevented customers from accessing the company Web site, while PIRT alone would respond to a mass mailing by the marketing department that used addresses without the appropriate level of permission).

Response Terms: Computer Emergency Response Team or CERT can be used interchangeably with CIRT, but CERT is a registered trademark of Carnegie Mellon University. Rather than call the privacy equivalent PERT, an acronym already used for a specific type of project management chart, I will use PIRT for Privacy Incident Response Team, or simply "incident response team." Also note that this section draws upon an article that I co-authored several years ago for *Infosecurity Magazine* titled "Incident Response and Recovery." My co-author was Michael Miora, CISSP, the founder of ContingenZ, a leading provider of incident management training and consulting services.

If there is one essential feature that distinguishes both the CIRT and the PIRT from other committees or groups within the company, it is readiness to act. The members of the PIRT must be available and on-call in emergency situations. They need to have the authority to make decisions in real time or, for extremely high-level decisions, get to the decision-maker quickly. A properly staffed PIRT, armed with the tools to solve the problems and record the results, can mean the difference between a minor incident that quickly disappears and a federal case that lasts for decades.

The make up of the PIRT will depend upon the size of your company and the business it is in. Clearly, some industries deal with more sensitive PII than others.

Basically, you want a group of people that includes management personnel with the authority to act, technical personnel with the skills needed to identify problems, legal personnel who are familiar with privacy law and any applicable regulations, and communications experts with the ability to report status in a posi-

tive manner. All team members should have above-average inter-
personal skills and be prepared to report to a team leader, chosen
for his or her above-average project management skills. Note that
the team leader is not necessarily the person that reports to the
media but the person who makes sure that the right person says the
right things to the right media.

The Privacy Incident Response Plan

The PIRT is guided by a Privacy Incident Response Plan (although
you could refer to this by the acronym PIRP, my preference is "the
incident response plan," the meaning of which is quite obvious
when used in the current context). The first item on the agenda
when creating a successful incident response plan is to identify
clearly when the response team should be activated. This means
determining what types of effects or incidents should cause escala-
tion from normal problem solving to emergency operations? A basic
question to ask is: who is authorized to determine that an emergency exists?

The incident response plan will then spell out the process for
activation of the PIRT, which requires contacting members of the
PIRT team and key management personnel. The plan must make
that process easy—the personnel working the problems already
have their hands full. There are automated systems that can, with
one simple command, start calling a tree-like structure with pre-
programmed messages for specific individuals. Speed is of the
essence, so a successful activation happens instantly after the event
and contacts the right people with the right information so they can
take action without delay.

There are many actions the team will take once the PIRT is
activated. Some of these actions will be technical—solve the problems and get things back to normal operations. Depending on the
type of incident, this may involve cooperation and coordination
with the CIRT. Other actions will be non-technical, and will include
public image actions, legal actions, and customer relations' actions.
These are just as important as the technical issues, so some members
of the team must be experts in those areas.

There are many steps the PIRT will take on its way to recovery
(see "Incident Response Steps"). No matter the intermediate step,

the last step is always to learn from the event. What lessons can the organization learn to make future emergencies less likely to occur, less sweeping in their consequences, and easier to recover from.The lessons learned step typically occurs at the end of a long day or week and so you might be tempted to skip it—don't! The loss of those lessons can doom the company to repeating its mistakes.

CERT Suggestions: To give you a sense of what is involved on the computer security side of things, here are some suggestions provided by the CERT Coordination Center:

1. Steps for determining if your system has been compromised:
    a. Look for modifications of system software and configuration files.
    b. Look for tools installed by the intruder.
    c. Similarly check other local systems.
    d. Check for systems at remote sites that may be involved or affected.

2. Steps for recovery from a system intrusion (assuming a Unix system):
    a. Regain control:
        - Disconnect from the network if necessary. Copy log files.
        - Review log files, check binaries & config files.
    b. Undo intruder modifications and install a clean system.
    c. Contact the sites identified in 1d above.

Seven Incident Response Steps

Here are the seven main steps to be taken by an incident response team. Note that the order and priority of steps may vary according to the specific needs of each organization and incident:

1. Identify that the situation calls for the PIRT to be activated, based on your organization's privacy incident response plan.

2. Make an initial determination of the nature and scope of the incident. For example, if you get a report that customer PII is exposed to the public due to a programming error on your Web site, you must verify the details ASAP. Is it one record or many records? Is the exposure blatant or is it dependent upon a high degree of skill?

3. Contact members of the PIRT team and key management personnel. Exactly who is contacted will depend upon the nature

and scale of the incident. For example, if there is blatant, large-scale exposure of PII, then someone who has the authority to halt systems should probably be among those contacted.

4. Take any defensive technical actions that will help contain the incident. For example, in the case of large-scale exposure of PII, temporary suspension of the site, or a portion of the site, may be indicated.

5. Solve any technical problems and get the system back to normal operations.

6. Execute non-technical actions:

a. public image actions, such as press releases, press interviews.

b. legal and law enforcement actions.

c. customer relations actions, such as reassuring clients, apologizing for shipping delays, etc.

d. reporting requirements, such as notifying parent company, partners, etc.

7. The last step is always to learn from the event.

Privacy Preparedness

As you put together your PIRT and develop your response plan it is perhaps natural to focus inwards. You will want to identify company personnel and resources that can be brought to bear in the event of an incident occurring. However, you should not neglect to establish the external relationships that can prove so vital in containing and recovering from an incident. These include:

• Local reporters, the people who cover your company for local and regional newspapers, as well as television and radio news reporters.

• National reporters for your industry segment (if you are a national company—most major networks have broad categories of coverage such as airlines, automotive, health, and so on).

• International and overseas media (if you are an international company you can expect international coverage of a major privacy incident as well as coverage in any country where you have an overseas presence, even if the incident did not occur in that country).

- Local, regional, national law enforcement (depending on the scale of the incident and your company's operations—it helps to know people in the attorney general's office, relevant state agencies, local FBI offices, and so on).

- Advocacy groups (consider a pre-emptive, pre-press briefing of any of the following that might be appropriate to the circumstances: EPIC, the Center for Digital Democracy, Center for Media Education, Computer Professionals for Social Responsibility, Consumer Action, Consumer Federation of America, Electronic Frontier Foundation, Junkbusters Corporation, Media Access Project, NetAction, Privacy Rights Clearinghouse, and the Children's Advertising Review Unit of the Better Business Bureau.

- Professional organizations (these include: privacy-specific groups such as the International Association of Privacy Officers; industry specific groups, such as the Information Technology Association Of America or the Consumer Task Force for Automotive Issues; and general industry groups, such as the Direct Marketing Association).

- Outside experts (people who specialize in incident management can bring cool heads and a wealth of experience to bear very quickly, and at a cost which may well be repaid many times over in terms of incident containment and damage control).

Like the costs of insurance or disaster recovery plans, the costs of preparing to handle a privacy incident can be hard to justify in standard return-on-investment terms. What privacy incident preparedness buys you is the assurance that, should an incident occur, the impact will be minimized. The mere existence of a PIRT with a plan, is evidence that your company takes privacy seriously—a factor of no small consequence when you come under the scrutiny of the FTC or attorneys general. First impressions count for a lot. If your response plan does nothing more than ensure that the right person speaks to the press or takes the call from the regulator, that alone may be worth the investment.

The alternatives—a crass comment from an ad hoc company spokesperson that lives forever in press coverage of the incident, or a defiant attitude that incites a regulator to make an example of your company—hardly bear thinking about.

CHAPTER EIGHT

PRIVACY AND EMAIL

01010110111001101111101001011100101010 11011011

"Spam, conventionally known as unsolicited commercial e-mail, is *the* No. 1 privacy-related complaint that consumers make to seal and certification program Truste. Nearly half, or 48 percent, of all complaints filed with us are spam-related. Consumers grumble that they are either unable to unsubscribe from email lists or believe that because they shared their email address with a Web site, they are getting unwanted mail."

—Fran Meier, executive director of Truste, *News.com Perspectives*, June, 2002.

8: PRIVACY
AND EMAIL

The company Web site and the company's use of email often go hand-in-hand. This chapter digs deeper into the relationship between Web sites, email, and privacy. In addition to surveying the current state of email as a business tool, I offer advice on respecting privacy in email and avoiding common business email snafus.

The Tangled Email Web

The power of the Web to transform businesses and empower consumers is matched only by the power of email, which is now a "mission-critical" application for most companies—plus a surprising number of families! In fact, if you ask a random sample of today's Internet users to cite their number one reason for going online, there's a good chance that more people will pick *checking email* than *surfing the Web.*

Email is likely to continue to be the Internet's number one application for many years because a lot of companies are only just starting to move their consumer communications to email—away from phone and snail mail—to lower the cost and improve the efficiency of customer relationship management (CRM) customer retention and not just for marketing.

However, while the person or department running the company Web site may not be the same person or department that sends out email to customers, the Web site is often the common link—the source of email addresses as well as the place where customer expectations are set, particularly with respect to privacy. And if there is one area of company activity that privacy advocates watch more closely than any other, it is email.

Email has been implicated in numerous privacy incidents, several of which have been discussed in previous chapters. This is perhaps not surprising, given the sheer volume of email today — global volume is expected to top 30 billion messages per day before the end of 2002! The chances of something going wrong, or someone making a mistake, are naturally quite high. However, you probably shouldn't try using that as an excuse when you have an irate customer on the line complaining about the single upsetting email you sent him!

The Spam Factor

The fact is, consumer patience with email issues has been worn very thin by large volumes of commercial email messages that are irrelevant and unwanted at best, offensive and fraudulent at worst. The vast majority of messages that fall into this category, commonly referred to as spam, are not sent by established companies with well-established brand names. Spam is typically sent by "fringe" companies and individuals seduced by hopes that email will enable them to "get rich quick."

How Rich, How Quick? If you're prepared to break the law you can make a lot of money selling false promises over the Internet. For example, you can buy bottles of "herbal" pills in bulk for $2.50 and resell them for $59.95, if you're prepared to swear they cause penis enlargement. Just put up a Web site with phony "before-and-after" photos and bogus testimonials; get a sleazy radio shock jock to talk you up; then send out millions of emails. That was the business plan of one Arizona company, and it proved *very* profitable, until it was busted by the State Attorney General, who seized some of those profits:

Nearly $3 million in cash plus a large amount of expensive jewelry.

More than $20 million in bank accounts.

Twelve luxury imported automobiles (including 8 Mercedes plus assorted models from Lamborghini, Rolls Royce, Ferrari and Bentley).

One office building and assorted luxury real estate in Paradise Valley and Scottsdale.

Indeed, spam is the all-round sucker's game. Send out 100 million messages touting a product for which you make fantastic claims and you may reel in enough suckers to make a profit. Send out enough messages touting a package of 100 million fresh email addresses for $79.95 and you may reel in enough suckers willing to buy (the fact that most of the addresses in such packages are useless does not seem to stop people buying or selling them).

Spam Not SPAM: The use of the word spam in the context of electronic messages stems from a sketch in the BBC television series *Monty Python* that depicted a restaurant menu upon which SPAM Luncheon Meat, produced by Hormel Foods Corporation, owner of the trademark SPAM, was featured prominently, and very repetitively. Personally, I quite like SPAM, but regardless of your personal palate, you must admire the way that Hormel has handled spam's passage into common usage. Rather than using corporate lawyers to fight it, Hormel let it happen, even creating some amusing Web pages about the phenomenon at www.spam.com. The company does stress that uppercase "SPAM" is still a trademark and you can't associate pictures of SPAM with spam. In any documents your company creates about spam, be sure to use the lowercase "spam."

The Economics of Spam

The sleazy side of email would be of no interest at all to legitimate companies and sensible consumers were in not for the fact that spam volumes have risen so dramatically in recent years that they threaten to overwhelm email systems, both personal and corporate, negating many of the benefits that have made email such a popular means of communication.

The underlying reasons for the continuing rise in spam volume can be found in the economics of the medium. Sending out millions of email messages costs the sender very little. An ordinary personal computer connected to the Internet via a $10 per month dial-up modem connection can pump out hundreds of thousands of messages a day; a small network of PCs connected via a $50 per month cable modem or DSL can churn out millions. As you can see, the economic barrier to entry into "get-rich-quick" spam schemes is very low. The risk of running into trouble with the authorities is also very low. The costs of spam are born downstream, in a number of ways, by several unwilling accomplices:

1. Recipients:

a. Spend time separating junk email from legitimate email. Unlike snail mail, which is typically delivered and sorted once per day, email arrives throughout the day, and night, and every time you check it you face the time-wasting distraction of having to sort out spam.

b. Pay to receive email. There are no free Internet connections. When you connect to the Internet somebody pays. The typical consumer at home pays a flat rate every month, but the level of that rate is determined, in part, by the volume of data that the Internet Service Provider handles, and spam inflates that volume, thus inflating cost.

2. Companies:

a. Lose productivity because employees, many of whom must check email for business purposes, are spending time weeding spam out of their company email in-box. Companies that allow employees to access personal email at work also get hit with time lost to personal spam weeding.

b. Waste resources because all that spam inflates bandwidth consumption, processing cycles, and storage space.

3. Internet Service Providers (ISPs), Email Service Providers (ESPs):

a. Waste resources on handling spam that inflates bandwidth consumption, processing cycles, and storage space.

b. Have to spend money on spam-filtering, block list administration, spam-related customer complaints, and filter/block-related complaints.

c. Have to devote resources to policing their users to avoid getting block-listed (there will be more about filters and block lists in the next section).

Two other economic factors in the rise of spam became evident towards the end of 2001: the recession; and declining delivery rates. When economic conditions take a turn for the worse, more people are willing to believe that get-rich-schemes are worth trying. As more and more spam filters are installed, some spammers have tried to compensate by simply sending more spam.

Until there is a major shift in the economics and technology of email, it will continue to present a virtual minefield for legitimate companies who want to employ this medium for customer communication or customer acquisition. On the one hand, your business risks upsetting email recipients who are frustrated by spam. On the other hand, your messages may not be delivered to the people who asked to receive them, thanks to anti-spam efforts.

Spam Filters and Block Lists

A complete discussion of spam filters, block lists, and other anti-spam technology, is beyond the scope of this book. What I have tried to include in this section is enough information for you to determine whether or not this technology is a cause of concern as your company develops its use of email for customer communication. If you think there is cause for concern, you can check out the additional sources at www.privacyforbusiness.com.

Relaying Trouble

You might be wondering why Internet Service Providers allow people to send spam. The fact is many do not. Spamming is a violation of just about every ISP's terms of service. Accounts used for spamming are frequently closed. However, there are some exceptions. As you might imagine, a few ISPs have decided to allow spam, as a way to get business (albeit business that nobody else wants). Some of these ISPs use facilities in fringe countries to avoid regulatory oversight.

Furthermore, some spammers find it easier, and cheaper, simply to steal service and use unauthorized access to other people's servers to send their messages. Which brings us to the phenomenon of mail relaying. According to Janusz Lukasiak of the University of Manchester, mail relaying occurs:

"when a mail server processes a mail message from an unauthorized external source with neither the sender nor the recipient being a local user. The mail server is an entirely unrelated third party to this transaction and the message has no business passing via the server."

How can this happen? In the early days of the Internet many servers were intentionally left "open" so that people could relay their email through them, simply for the sake of convenience. Abuse of this arrangement by spammers has required the standard for acceptable use to change. However, mail relaying continues to occur because configuring servers to prevent it requires effort, and spammers keep finding new ways to exploit resources that are not totally protected. For example, port 25 filtering, instituted to reduce spamming, is now being bypassed with tricks like asynchronous routing and proxies.

The Old Days: In the early days of the Internet it was quite acceptable for individuals to send their email through just about any mail server, since the impact on resources was minimal. If you have used the Internet for more than a few years you may recall a time when you could connect to the net via one ISP and send messages through a server belonging to another ISP. Abuses by spammers, who do impact resources, led to ISPs instituting restrictions, such as requiring you to log in to the POP server to collect your incoming mail before sending any out (since that requires a user name and password it prevents "strangers" from sending email through the server).

Thus there is a war being fought on the fringes of the Internet, between spammers and ISPs. Although it might seem to you that your own personal in-basket is the front line in the fight against spam, your ISP will tell you it's just a skirmish compared to the battle it is waging. So imagine what things are like at your ISP's ISP. That's not a typo—most Internet Service Providers actually get their service from an even larger service provider, companies like Genuity and Worldcom. How much trouble do these companies have with spam? Consider the number of trouble tickets that network abuse (spam) generates each month at Worldcom: 350,000! You can bet that these companies are working hard to prevent things like mail relaying and defeat the latest tricks that spammers have devised to get around those preventative measures.

Black Holes

One spam fighting weapon does not rely on the escalating technology of port filtering. Black hole lists or block lists simply catalogue server IP addresses from ISPs whose customers are deemed responsible for spam and from ISPs whose servers are hijacked for spam relay. ISPs and companies subscribe to these lists to find out from which IP addresses to block traffic. The receiving end, such as the consumer recipient's ISP, checks the list for the connecting IP address. If the IP address matches one on the list, then the connection gets dropped before accepting any traffic. Other ISPs choose simply to ignore or "black hole" IP packets at their routers. Among the better known block lists are MAPS Realtime Blackhole List (MAPS RBL), Spamcop, ORDB, ORBZ, SPEWS, and Spamhaus.

How do ISPs get on these lists? If an ISP openly permits spam, or does not adequately protect its resources against abuse by spammers, it will likely be reported to the list by one or more recipients of such spam. Reports are filed by people who take the time to examine the spam's header, identify the culpable ISP and make a "nomination" to a block list. Different block lists have different standards for verifying nominations. Some test the nominated server, others take into account the number of nominations. If an ISP, or company or individual operating a mail server, finds themselves on the list by mistake, they can request to be removed, which usually involves a test by the organization operating the block-list.

Note that none of this block-list policing of spam is "official." All block lists are self-appointed and self-regulated. They set, and enforce, their own standards. The only recourse for entities who feel they have been unfairly blocked, and there have been plenty of these lately, is legal action. Some block lists are operated outside of the United States, but if an overseas organization block-lists a server located in the United States it can probably be sued in a US court. However, it is important to note that the blocking is not done by the operator of the block list, it is done by ISPs who subscribe to, and are guided by, the lists. Later I will discuss the implications of this situation for corporate email campaigns.

Spam Filters

Block list systems filter out messages from a certain domain or IP address, or range of IP addresses; they do not examine the content of messages. Filtering out spam based on content can be done at several levels and began at the client level. Many email users actually perform a reverse filter for spam. For example, I have separate mailboxes into which I filter all of the messages I get from my usual correspondents, friends, family, colleagues, subscribed newsletters, and so on. That means whatever is left in my in-basket is spam, with the notable exception of messages from new correspondents for whom I have not yet created a separate mailbox and filter.

To perform a positive filter for spam you need to identify elements common to spam messages. There are now a variety of products that do that, such as the aggressively-named SpamKiller from McAfee. The default set of filters that SpamKiller installs will look for things like "From" addresses that contain a lot of numbers and "Subject" text that contains a lot of punctuation characters—spammers often add in an attempt to defeat filters based on specific text, so the Subject line "You're Approved" might be randomly concatenated with special characters like this:

> "**You're Approved**"

Unfortunately, some of the language you find in spam also appears in legitimate messages, such as "You are receiving this message because you subscribed to this list" or "To unsubscribe, click here." This means that the default filtering in a product like SpamKiller is likely to block some messages that you want to get. The answer is to either weaken the filtering or create a "white list" of legitimate "From" addresses so that the spam filter will allow through anything from these addresses. Most personal spam filters can read your address book and add all of the entries to your personal white list.

ISPs have been reluctant to conduct content-based spam filtering, fearing that it might be construed as reading other people's email and lead to claims of privacy invasion. However, because ISPs must be able to read headers to route email, some have been prepared to filter on the "Subject" field, hence the attempts by spammers to randomly vary Subject text. Furthermore, some ISPs have found that distaste for spam has now reached the level at which some users are prepared to accept revised terms of agreement that allow machine reading of email content to perform spam filtering.

Sticky legal issues still exist for ISPs however, especially since there is no generally accepted definition of spam, and no consensus of the extent to which freedom of speech applies to email. For example, do political candidates have a right to send unsolicited email to constituents? Do ISPs have a right to block it? These are questions on which the courts of law and public opinion have yet to render a verdict.

One place where content-based spam filters are being deployed with little or no concern for legal challenges is the corporate network. Based on the fact that the company network belongs to the company, the right to control how it is used trumps concerns over privacy. Employees do not have the right to receive, at work, whatever kind of email they want to receive. And most companies would argue that there is virtually no corporate obligation to deliver email to employees. So what do companies that send email to customers need to know? Whether you email customers at home or at work, poor message design can, as discussed later in this chapter, result in legitimate messages being blocked by spam filters at any of three levels: ISP, corporate, and end-user.

The Size of Spam

Another statement about email upon which most companies and many consumers can agree is that spam has grown from a mere annoyance to a huge burden. In all likelihood, the only people who will disagree with this assessment are consumers that haven't been using email for very long and companies that send spam.

How big is the burden? In my assessment spam threatens to seriously undermine the benefits of the Internet. Before discounting that assessment as extreme, bear in mind that by the time you read this, more than half of all email traffic on the Internet will more than likely be spam. In August of 2002, three different email service providers indicated that spam could make up the majority of message traffic on the Internet by the end of the year (as reported by CNET, the Internet news service). The three sources—Brightmail, Postini, and MessageLabs—provide spam filtering and interception services for companies. Brightmail's interception figures for July showed that unsolicited bulk email made up a 36 percent of all email traveling over the Internet, up from 8 percent a year ago.

Postini found that spam made up 33 percent of its customers' email in the same month, up from 21 percent in January. MessageLabs reported that its customers were now classifying from 35 percent to more that 50 percent of their email traffic as spam.

At those growth rates, the point at which spam will overtake legitimate email is fast approaching. In fact, in September of 2002, Microsoft indicated to the press that 80 percent of the email that passes through its servers is "junk." This includes a staggering 1 billion spam messages received, per day, by holders of Hotmail accounts.

All the anecdotal evidence I have heard tells the same story. Furthermore, as the owner of the cobb.com domain I have some spam statistics of my own. During a 15 month period, starting in 2001 and going into 2002, I recorded a remarkably consistent month-to-month spam volume increase of 10 percent.

The burden on ISPs and company mail servers is enormous. A Postini study earlier in 2002 indicated that 53 percent of email server processing time is wasted on junk email and email attacks. Consider the effect on infrastructure spending. Storage is one of the biggest hardware and maintenance costs that ISPs bear. If half of all email is spam then ISPs are spending twice as much as they need to on storage.

The productivity "hit" for companies whose employees waste time weeding spam out of their in-baskets is also enormous. Gartner has estimated that a company of 10,000 employees suffers more than $13 million worth of lost productivity—from internally generated spam alone.

The big fear is that spam could actually put the brakes on Internet growth rates, which would have a negative effective on those economies, such as America's, that currently derive considerable strength from Internet-related goods and services. Perhaps the only reason such an effect has not yet been felt is that spam's impact on new users is limited. In other words, when new users first get email addresses they typically don't get a lot of spam. According to some studies, it can take six to twelve months for spammers to find an email address, but when they do, the volume of spam to that address can increase very quickly.

Email and Privacy

The inadvertent exposure by Eli Lilly of email addresses belonging to people who had registered at the prozac.com Web site highlighted a number of important facts about email, Web sites, and privacy:

1. An email address can be considered personally identifiable information.

2. An email address can be considered *sensitive* personally identifiable information in certain contexts, such as association with a particular Web site (this "sensitive" distinction was discussed in Chapter 2 with reference to the DoubleClick case).

3. If the employees who manage email are not aware of how sensitive it can be, they may not handle it with enough care (if the operation of the prozac.com email program had been adequately tested, using fake data, the error would have been caught, before it exposed real data).

4. The employees who manage email are likely to be part of the Internet side of the company, which includes the Web site, which means they may not be bound by, or accustomed to standard IT safeguards and protocols—such as version management and quality control—which exist to prevent untested code entering production.

5. You don't need to compromise the privacy of many people to bring down a lot of regulatory scrutiny (only a handful of the email addresses revealed in the prozac.com mailing were "directly identifiable" like stephen.cobb@stephencobb.com as opposed to cobbs99@aol.com).

All of the above have been widely discussed in the privacy literature, but several other serious lessons have been largely overlooked in discussions of the Prozac Email Incident. While the FTC investigation focused attention on the one inadvertent disclosure that was due to a programming error at Lilly, there was a potentially much larger and more serious risk of disclosure during the entire time that the Prozac reminder service was in operation.

Think about people reading email at work—typically this is done via the company network, even when people check their personal email over the Web and don't use a company email address. How much confidentiality does such email enjoy? The answer is virtually none. The possibilities that messages could be seen by someone other than the intended recipient are nearly endless. Consider these scenarios:

- a network administrator running a packet inspector;

- a sysadmin backing up the mail server or a workstation;

- a technician repairing a crashed system;

- a leased computer going back to the vendor;

- a co-worker "borrowing" someone's workstation.

During the last five years, all of the above have been cited in lawsuits involving compromised email. The ethics of reading another person's email are one thing, the probability of it happening is another. The point is, whether messages are company email or Web email, when they pass through the company network they are potentially visible to other people on the network; and if you read email on your computer traces will remain on your computer — unless your technical skills and paranoia level are way above average.

What about email encryption, the technology which enables you to scramble the content of messages you send so that only people to whom you give a "key" can unscramble and read it? The fact is, very few people today are encrypting their email.

HIPAA and Email Encryption: The proposed HIPAA Security Rule effectively outlaws the use of unencrypted Internet email for personally identifiable medical information.

Furthermore, and this is what many people seemed to have overlooked in the Prozac Email Incident, most forms of email encryption do not encrypt the headers. So even if you got an encrypted message from prozac.com, someone could still see that you had received a message of some sort from prozac.com. The message for companies is clear: email traffic itself can constitute sensitive PII, and email is not yet ready for some forms of communication, even if they are executed without a hitch.

Email Headers

The scenario of a privacy incident in Chapter 7 included some discussion of email headers. This section covers the subject in more detail—although nowhere near exhaustively—to give you an idea of what to look forward to when exploring email-related privacy issues. Email cannot be delivered without headers and every email message has one, a section of the message that is not always displayed in the recipient's email program, but is there nonetheless, describing where the message came from, how it was addressed, and how it was delivered. Examining the header can tell you a lot about a message.

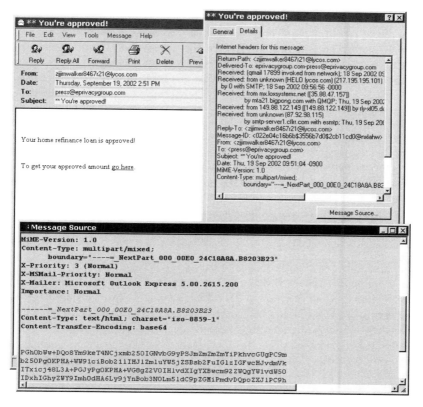

Figure 8-1: Viewing message header details in Outlook Express

Consider how a message appears in Microsoft Outlook Express. At the top you can see the "From" and the "To" and the "Subject." For example, in Figure 8-1, on the preceding page, you can see part of a message that appears to be from zjjimwalker8467r21@lycos.com to press@eprivacygroup.com with the subject: *You're approved!

The entire content of this message appears to be a few sentences. You can't see them all in Figure 8-1 but they read:

"Your home refinance loan is approved!

"To get your approved amount go here.

"To be excluded from further notices go here."

You have probably figured out that press@eprivacygroup.com is not a real person. This is just an address that appears on my employer's Web site as a contact for the press (the idea being that press inquiries received via email can be routed to different people at different times, depending on who is assigned press duty). And of course, nobody actually used this address for a mortgage. The address was picked up by a "harvesting" program that automatically scours the Web for email addresses that can be sold to suckers or scam artists.

When you open this message in Outlook Express and use the File/Properties command, you can click on the Details tab to see how the message made its way through the Internet. The first thing you see is a box labeled headers, as shown in Figure 8-1. Reading this will tell you that the message was routed through several different email servers.

Qmail is my company's mail program, which is the first instance of "Received." The next three below that are intermediaries, until you get to the last one, smtp-server1.cflrr.com. That is an email server in Central Florida (cfl) on the Road Runner (rr) cable modem network, which supplies high speed Internet access to tens of thousands of households.

So who sent this message? That is very hard to say. As you might expect, there is no such address as zjjimwalker8467r21 at lycos.com. The best way to determine who sent a spam message like this is to examine the content. Spam cannot reel in suckers unless there is some way for the suckers to contact the spammer. Sometimes this is a phone number, but in this message it is a hyperlink to a Web page. However, clicking links in spam messages is a dangerous way to surf—a much safer technique is message source inspection. Outlook Express provides a Message Source view, but this may only show the encoded content and not be readable ASCII.

A trick I use to get at the content of such messages is to forward them to a different email client, for example Qualcomm's Eudora, then open the mailbox file with a text editor such as TextPad. This reveals the "http" reference for the link that this spammer wants the recipient to click. In this case, the sucker who clicks on the link that says "To get your approved amount go here" is presented with a form, part of which is shown in Figure 8-2. This form gathers exactly the kind of information you would want to have if you were going to defraud someone.

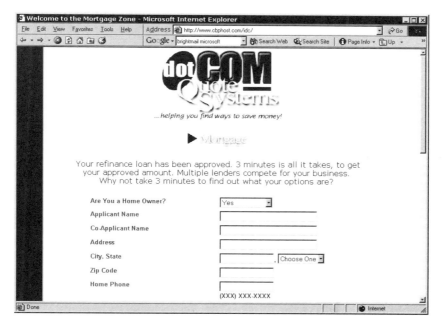

Figure 8-2: Mortgage scam form

That's right, this message is not about mortgages, but about data gathering. To what use the data thus gathered will be put is impossible to say, but a little additional checking using the *ping* and *whois* commands reveals that the Web server collecting the data is in Beijing, China! The chances of finding out who set it up are slim. The standard operating procedure for these scams is to set up and take down each server very quickly, gathering as much data as you can before someone starts to investigate.

The risk of investigation increases with the volume of spam sent. For example, the same press@eprivacygroup.com address received at least 5 of these "You're Approved" messages within a 30-day period, all from some variation of "zjjimwalker" at Lycos or Yahoo. Someone managing a larger number of email accounts might have received hundreds. At some point the volume moves some people to action.

Who would investigate something like this? Fortunately, there is a small army of anti-spam investigators out there. Visit the news.admin.net-abuse.email newsgroup and you will find them (tip: you can use Google Groups to search and read this newsgroup in your Web browser). Many work for ISPs, filtering companies and block lists. You can learn a lot from these people and any company considering email as a customer communication channel should spend time monitoring that newsgroup. Bear in mind that some people have been fighting spam for a long time and their views have hardened. Their positions sometimes may seem a bit extreme.

Spam and Privacy

Regardless of what you think about spam, it is clear that few things tarnish a company's reputation with consumers these days quicker than accusations of spamming. You only have to listen to the language used when the subject comes up in conversation, even in a public forum. For example, the phrase "We need a public hanging" was used by several speakers at an anti-spam conference I attended in June of 2002, hosted by the Global Internet Project, which is "an international group of senior executives committed to fostering continued growth of the Internet," and not a gang of radicals.

But what does spam have to do with privacy? If you ask Fran Meier, executive director of TRUSTe, she will tell you that consumers "definitely consider spam an intrusion on their privacy." This is not surprising if you remember that one of the most frequently quoted definitions of privacy is: "the state of being free from unwanted intrusion." Although a lot of people disagree about how privacy should be defined, one statement upon which most companies and many consumers can agree is that spam definitely counts as unwanted intrusion.

Many would also agree that spam violates another aspect of privacy, control over the use of information pertaining to oneself, namely, one's email address. Unlike most physical addresses, email addresses often include personal elements such as one's name. Many people feel that they own their email address, and that it identifies them, much more than their physical address does. That combined sense of ownership and identity probably goes a long way to explain why we get so much more upset about junk email than about junk snail mail.

Taking the Abuse: One Web site strategy you might consider is setting up a form for people to complain about spam. The thinking behind this strategy is that complaints about spam sent by your company are almost inevitable—whether or not justified is another matter. So, instead of waiting for them to reach whatever random part of the organization the offended party contacts, which may or may not know how to handle them, provide a central collection point to manage them. By providing a link on the company Web site that allows people to send you their complaints you achieve several goals:

1. People who are upset about your alleged spam will not be further frustrated by trying to find how to bring it to someone's attention.

2. You can design the form to capture a lot of useful information about the alleged spam, in a standard format that fits your needs, as opposed to gleaning the facts from a letter or fax composed by the offended party.

3. You can use the form to stress your company's commitment to responsible email practices. For example, you might put "Your Company does not condone unsolicited bulk email. If you feel you have received such email from us, please use the following form to report it and we will take action."

To complete the spam-privacy-Web site circle, think about what people do when they are upset. They complain. When people are sitting at their computer and get upset by spam, they use their computer to complain. When consumers get messages that they consider spam, from companies that have had their Web site privacy policies certified by TRUSTe, they complain to TRUSTe. You can tell a lot about the spam-privacy-Web site connection from the fact that complaints about spam outnumbered all others received by TRUSTe.

The Anti-Spam Perspective

There are three things you need to know about spam if your company plans to use email to communicate with customers, current or prospective.

1. **Some people get very upset when they receive spam.** If they get email from you that they judge to be spam, they can be very vocal in their objections.

2. **There is no universal definition of spam.** No laws or regulations define spam, which is truly "in the eye of the beholder." In other words, if someone thinks the email you sent them is spam, it is assumed to be spam, until proven otherwise (if this strikes you as unreasonable, remember the truth of the old adage: the customer is always right).

3. **Some spam blocking systems block legitimate messages.** Because there is not, nor will there ever be, a universally-accepted definition of spam, systems that attempt to block spammers or filter out spam messages will sometimes block legitimate messages, which can undermine the effectiveness of email for legitimate purposes.

The problem that legitimate users of email face right now is that the abuse of the Internet by spammers has so inflamed some people they have adopted quite extreme positions. For example, some people will say it is acceptable to block all email from a particular ISP if one person uses that ISP to send out spam.

Blocking a company's newsletter to its customers is considered, by some, to be an acceptable price to pay for the overall benefits of such measures, even though the people who didn't get the newsletter specifically asked to receive it. There is something inherently unfair about this situation, this inflcting of collateral damage on innocent people—those who send legitimate messages that never get delivered and those who fail to get the mail they were expecting.

Anti-Spam's Collateral Damage: If you search the Web you will find many examples of legitimate messages getting zapped by spam filters and black holes, but this one is personal. My father-in-law, who lives about 90 miles away, called me one day to say his email to my wife—his daughter—was being rejected. This is a man who used to design tank simulators and wrote DOS batch files for his PC long before Windows arrived, so I was pretty sure this was not a case of user error.

On the other hand, it was hard to see why the message could not get through. My father-in-law forwarded the rejected messages to me and it appeared that my wife's ISP was denying her very existence. At the same time, my wife was not having trouble getting mail from other people.

Then we heard from her sister, who lives just a few miles from their father. She called to say that her email to my wife had also been rejected. Since uses the same ISP as he does, namely Road Runner cable modem service, a common thread was emerging. Could my wife's ISP be blocking all email from all Road Runner users?

Not exactly, but they were blocking all email from cfl.rr.com, which is the Central Florida portion of the Road Runner service, used by thousands of households. Now think back to the spam examined earlier in the chapter. It came through cfl.rr.com! That's why this particular domain was "black-holed" and thousands of legitimate email users had their messages blocked for weeks—some ISPs would rather do that than allow spam to get through.

Responsible Email

Email that is not spam is used by many legitimate companies to communicate with customers. This is customer dialogue conducted via email, and marketing messages sent to people who have opted to receive them. Typical examples are the messages I get every month from my credit card company telling me that my latest statement is available for my perusal at the company Web site, or the messages I get each week from my favorite airline telling me about special airfares available on the company's Web site.

Like the email reminder service operated by Lilly, these examples illustrate the complex relationship that often exists among Web sites, email, and privacy. Many Web sites ask visitors for their email addresses. In Chapter 6 you learned how to bracket such requests with a suitable privacy notice, but it is also important that someone within the organization take responsibility for upholding the terms of such notice. For example, someone needs to tell the marketing department that there are limits on the type and frequency of messages that can be sent to these addresses. Someone must make sure management understands that, unless specifically stated in the Web site privacy statement, these email addresses cannot be sold or traded to another company; even if your company is faced with bankruptcy and wants to consider these addresses a disposable asset.

Six Email Resolutions

If you want a starting point for your efforts to make sure your company is associated with responsible email practices, you should become familiar with the "Six Resolutions for Responsible Emailers." These were created by the Council for Responsible Email (CRE), which was formed under the aegis of the Association for Interactive Marketing (AIM), a subsidiary of the Direct Market Association (DMA). Some of the country's largest companies, and largest legitimate users of email, belong to these organizations, and they have a vested interest in making sure that email is not abused. Here are the six resolutions::

- Marketers must not falsify the sender's domain name or use a non-responsive IP address without implied permission from the recipient or transferred permission from the marketer.

- Marketers must not purposely falsify the content of the subject line or mislead readers from the content of the email message.

- All bulk email marketing messages must include an option for the recipient to unsubscribe (be removed from the list) from receiving future messages from that sender, list owner, or list manager.

- Marketers must inform the respondent at the time of online collection of the email address for what marketing purpose the respondent's email address will be used.

- Marketers must not harvest email addresses with the intent to send bulk unsolicited commercial email without consumers' knowledge or consent. (*Harvest* is defined as compiling or stealing email addresses through anonymous collection procedures such as via a Web spider, through chat rooms, or other publicly displayed areas listing personal or business email addresses.)

• The CRE opposes sending bulk unsolicited commercial email to an email address without a prior business or personal relationship. (*Business or personal relationship* is defined as any previous recipient-initiated correspondence, transaction activity, customer service activity, third-party permission use, or proven offline contact.)

These six resolutions strike me as a fairly reasonable middle ground between the anti-spam and marketing extremists (credit for this broad consensus must go to the people who helped craft the resolutions, including my colleague, James Koenig). If everyone abided by these resolutions, there would be no spam, at least according to most people's definition of spam. After all, if nobody received more than one or two unwanted and irrelevant messages per week, anti-spam sentiment would cool significantly.

The Append Issue

Some privacy advocates have objected to the sixth resolution because it permits email appending. This is the practice of finding an email address for a customer who has not yet provided one, offered as a business service by companies such as Yesmail and AcquireNow. For example, if you are a bank, you probably have physical addresses for all your customers, but you may not have email addresses for all of them. You can hire a firm like AcquireNow to find email addresses for customers who have not provided one. However, these customers may not have given explicit permission for the bank to contact them via email, so some people would say that sending email messages to them is spamming.

Whether or not you agree with that assessment, several factors need to be considered carefully if your company is considering using an email append service. First of all, you had better make sure that nothing in your privacy policy forbids it. Next you want to think hard about the possible reaction from customers, bearing in mind that email appending is not a perfect science (for more on how appending works, simply enter "email append" as a search term in

Google—you will find a lot of companies offering to explain how they do it, matching data pulled from many different sources using complex algorithms).

Another concern that must considered is that some messages will go to people who are not customers. For that reason, you probably want to make your first contact a tentative one, such as a polite request to make further contact. Then you can formulate the responses to build a genuine opt-in list. As you might expect, you can outsource this entire process to the append service, which will have its own, often automated, methods of dealing with bounced messages, complaints, and so on.

Note that you probably don't want to include any sensitive personal information in the initial contact, since you have no guarantee that bob.jones@majorfreemail.net is the Robert Jones you have on your customer list.

When Citibank did an append mailing in the summer of 2002, encouraging existing customers to use the bank's online account services, it came in for some serious criticism. Although the bank was not providing immediate online access to appended customers, the mere perception of this, combined with a number of mistaken email identities, produced negative publicity.

Citibank Append Questions? Here's what Citibank said in the message it sent to people it believed to be customers, even though these people had not provided their email address directly to the bank:

"Citibank would like to send you email updates to keep you informed about your Citi Card, as well as special services and benefits...With the help of an email service provider, we have located an email address that we believe belongs to you."

While this message is certainly polite, it clearly raised questions in the minds of recipients. Two questions which could undermine appending as a business practice are: "Where exactly is this service provider looking for these email addresses?" and "Why doesn't the company that wants my email address just write and ask for it?" The fact is, conversion rates from email contact are higher than from snail mail, so the argument for append services is that companies who use them move more quickly to the cheaper and better medium of email than those that don't. The counterpoint is that too many people will be offended in the process.

You should also consider to what lengths you are stretching the "prior business relationship" principle cited in the sixth responsible email resolution. A bank probably has a stronger case for appending email addresses to its account holder list than a mail order company that wants to append a list of people who requested last year's catalogue. The extent to which privacy advocates accept or decry the concept of "prior business relationship" is largely dependent upon how reasonable companies are in their interpretation of it.

Problems With Email

Of course, there will always be some companies that stretch the rules, and others that ignore them altogether. That leads some anti-spammers to condemn all companies in the same breath. My own experience, working with large companies that have respected brand names, is that none of them actually want to offend consumers. Some big companies may be struggling to rein in maverick email marketing activities, but upper management is clearly opposed to anything that could be mistaken for spamming.

Not that the motives for corporate responsibility in email are purely altruistic. Smart companies can see that the perpetuation of disreputable email tactics only dilutes the tremendous potential of email as a business tool. The next few sections look at some of the ways in which bad email, and the battle against it, can impact your company's use of email.

Filtering Problems

Anti-spam measures are now deployed by many ISPs, companies, and consumers, as described earlier in the chapter in the section "Spam Filters and Block Lists." These measures sometimes produce "false positives," flagging legitimate email as spam, potentially preventing your email from reaching the intended recipients, even when they have asked to receive your email.

If your company's email is deemed to be particularly egregious spam, the server through which it is sent is likely to be blocked. If this is your company's general email server, blocking could affect delivery of a lot more than just the "spam." If the servers through which your large mailing is sent belong to a service provider, and its servers get blocked, that could be a problem for you too. And if you use a service provider to execute the mailing for you but don't choose wisely, your mail may be branded as spam just because of the bad reputation of the servers through which it passes.

What can be done to prevent messages that are not spam from falling victim to anti-spam measures? Adherence to responsible email practices is a good first step. Responsible management of the company's email servers will also help, as will selection of reputable service providers.

You should also consider tasking someone with tracking anti-spam measures, to make sure that your email is designed to avoid, as much as possible, any elements of content or presentation that are currently being flagged as spam. Beyond this, there are some new initiatives emerging to address the false positive problem, notably by creating universal "white lists." There will be more on this in the next chapter.

You've Got Bogus Email

Bogus email can be defined as "email designed to look like it came from, was sent on behalf of, or is otherwise endorsed by, someone other than actual the sender." This includes email where the "From" address is spoofed in the header as well as email that uses a company name or brand name for commercial purposes without permission, particularly when such use would tend to dilute the value of said name. Examples are numerous and multiplying fast:

> "Bogus emails traded on Amazon's name"
> —News & Observer, August 28, 2002

> "The State Department's email identity was forged by a computer virus that sent itself to law enforcement and media outlets across the country"
> —Associated Press, May. 21, 2002

> "Spammers are also increasingly forging mail headers, a tactic known as spoofing, to make email appear to come from legitimate sources. US corporations including Bank of America, eBay and Wells Fargo have fallen victim to junk mailers taking free rides on their names."
> —ZDNet, March 21, 2002

At my company we filter out a lot of unwanted email to a "spam bucket." Recently we found examples of bogus email in the spam bucket that used the following brand names: MSNBC, Discover, Viagra, Norton, and Capital One. The problems caused by bogus email range from time-wasting to serious security breaches and privacy violations, not to mention the costly impact of brand dilution, which can adversely affect not only companies but also professional associations and non-profit groups.

Solving the problem is difficult because of the huge imbalance of risk and cost between the perpetrators and the victims. Spoofing an email header takes mere seconds. Sending hundreds of thousands of bogus messages takes mere minutes. Finding out who sent them can take hours. Preventing people from sending more is nigh on impossible, despite the availability of numerous legal sanctions that could be applied, if you could find the offender. Given the global nature of the Internet, shutting down such operations is a jurisdictional nightmare, and there appears to be an endless supply of persons willing to try their hand at the bogus email game.

Instead of trying to stop people sending bogus mail, the best solution may be the establishment of spoof-proof credentials for legitimate email. That is what a technology called Postiva does. Because it can place a cryptographically secure authentication stamp in each outbound message, Postiva enables organizations to positively identify legitimate email while at the same time disavowing any and all email that is not stamped. There will be more about Postiva in the next chapter, but the point is that companies, charities, and government agencies would all benefit if they could tell recipients of their email not to accept, act upon, or put stock in, any messages that are not stamped messages. An enormous reduction in confusion, liability, and brand degradation would result.

Email Precautions

Whatever you think of spam, there is no denying that, as a business tool, bulk email is incredibly powerful. It is also very seductive. When you have a story to tell or a product to sell, and a big list of email addresses just sitting there, bulk email can be very tempting. You can find yourself thinking "Where's the harm?" and "Who's going to object?" But unless you have documented permission to send your message to the people on that list, the smart business decision is to resist the temptation. Remember, it only takes one recipient suitably offended to ruin your day.

Let's Test Again

One of the most basic business email precautions is this: Never send a message unless you are sure you know what it will look like to the person who receives it. This covers the formatting, the language you use, and above all, the addressing. If you want to address the same message to more than one person at a time, you have four options, each of which should be handled carefully.

If you place the email addresses of all recipients in the "To" field, or place one or more in the "Cc" field, all the recipients will be able to see the addresses of the other people to whom you sent the message. This is sometimes appropriate for communications within a small group of people, but if the number of people in the group exceeds about 20, or if you do *not* want everyone to know who is getting the message, move all but one of them to the "Bcc" field.

If the disclosure of recipients is likely to cause any embarrassment whatsoever, do a test mailing first. Send a copy of the message to yourself and at least one colleague outside the company, and then have them look at the message to make sure the "Bcc" entries were made correctly.

Use the Right Software

Somewhere between a precaution and a recommendation is using the right email software for the job. There are mature applications that can reliably build individual, customized messages to each person on a list. This neatly sidesteps errors related to the "To" and "Cc" fields. In Figure 8-3 you can see an example of such an application, Group Mail Pro.

Group Mail Pro stores email addresses in a database and builds messages on the fly using a merge feature like a word processor. You can insert database fields in the message. For example, a message can refer to the recipient by name. The program also offers extensive testing of messages, so that you can see what recipients will see, before you send any messages. You can also apply a wide range of filters when sending messages. The program has the ability to send messages in small groups, spread over time, according the abilities of your Internet connection.

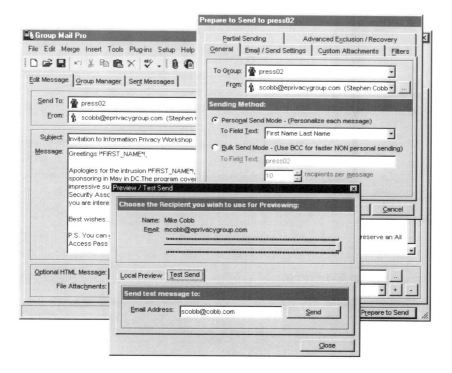

Figure 8-3 Group Mail Pro

Cool Tool or Spam Machine? The fact that a powerful, professional-level email program also sounds a lot like a spamming machine is just another example of technology's double-edged sword. Some spammers undoubtedly use such software. However, as someone who has used this same software for years to improve communications with students in my online training classes, I would resent the implication that spamming is the only thing such programs are used for.

Whether you use a commercial email program like Group Mail, or something even more powerful, depends upon several factors, such as the size of your organization, the number of messages you need to send, and your privacy policy. That's right, privacy comes into play here because some software used to send email allows the user of the program access to the database containing the addresses to which the mail is being sent.

This is generally not a problem in smaller companies, or when the database consists solely of names and addresses without any special context; but it can be an issue when the database contains sensitive information or the context is sensitive. For example, a list of names and addresses can be sensitive if the person handling the list knows, or can infer, that they to belong to patients undergoing a certain kind of medical treatment.

You may not want to allow system operators or programmers to have access to sensitive data simply because they are charged with sending or programming messages to people. Fortunately, mailing programs can be written that allow an operator to compose mail and send it, without seeing the names and addresses of the people to whom it is being sent. Test data can, and should, be used to "proof" the mailing before it is executed.

Know Your Audience

Another basic email precaution is: Do your best never to send any message that might offend any of the recipients. In choosing your wording, your design, your message, know your audience. Use particular caution when it comes to humor, politics, religion, sex, or any other sensitive subject. When using email for business purposes you can bet that it is better to stand accused of a lack of humor than a lack of judgment.

Respect people's preferences, if you know them, for content. If people have expressed a preference for text-only messages, don't send them html and hope they decide to change their minds. Ask first because the "forgiveness later" path is not cost-effective when you have to deal with thousands of unhappy recipients.

And as a general rule, when you do use html content, try to keep size to a minimum, unless you have recipients who specifically requested large, media-rich, bandwidth hungry, disk-hogging messages.

Something to Think About: The head of marketing asks you to send her a file of email addresses that have been input on the technical support registration page of your company's Web site. What do you do?

Obviously, a detailed answer will depend upon the exact nature of your company's organizational structure, but since you have been reading this chapter you know enough to ask what use marketing intends to make of these addresses. Suppose the answer is "include them in the mailing list for an email marketing campaign." You would be well advised to suggest that the company review the form on which the addresses were submitted and the Web site's privacy statement.

Marketing to addresses that were not supplied with a clear understanding that they would be used for such purposes is not advisable. Depending upon your privacy statement, it could be violation of your company's privacy policy. Going ahead with such a violation could not only annoy customers, but it could draw the attention of industry regulators, such as the FTC. Of course, you will have to decide for yourself if it is your job or responsibility to point this out to management.

And be sure to provide a simple way for recipients to opt out of any further mailings. (A link to a Web form is best for this—avoid asking the recipient to reply to the message—if the email address to which you mailed the message is no longer their primary address, they may have trouble opting out with a simple reply.)

Always get as much assurance as you can that the people on the list actually opted to be on the list. Always include a preemptive apology, such as "We apologize if you received this message in error." Perhaps the easiest bulk email mistake to make is to assume that all the people on the list actually belong there.

Unless you have been practicing good "data hygiene" you may find that a list contains addresses that were inappropriately included. Any steps you can take to find this out before using the list are probably worth taking, because finding it out from several thousand angry message recipients is no fun.

How do mistakes like this happen? Carelessness and failure to follow strict procedures are often the cause, but deception can play a part too. If you buy or rent a list you have to be careful you buy from a reputable source. If you acquire a list through other means, such as a business deal, you may want more than just the verbal assurance of the party who supplied the list that it is suitable for the purposes claimed. Just as you should document and track internal list compilation, you should ask for documentation from anyone who supplies you with a list. Hopefully, this will show where and under what circumstances the names were added to the list, as well as what privacy policies governed their collection and what permissions were provided. If you can't get suitable assurances that adequate permission was given for the uses to which you plan to put the list, it is better to resist temptation and take a different path.

CHAPTER NINE

TOOLS, SEALS, TECHNIQUES

01010110111001101111101001011100101010110110 11

"Anyone today who thinks the privacy issue has peaked is greatly mistaken…we are in the early stages of a sweeping change in attitudes that will fuel political battles and put once-routine business practices under the microscope."

—Forrester Research, March 5, 2001.

9: Tools, Seals, Techniques

By now it should be clear that privacy for business Web sites is no small challenge. Fortunately, help is available, due in part to the fact that entrepreneurs tend to see challenges as opportunities and so commercial tools to help Web sites meet the privacy challenge are starting to appear on the market. In this chapter I discuss some of these tools, as well as the role of trade associations and non-profit groups; several of which offer guidance and guidelines to help Web sites comply with privacy best practices. Web privacy seals, like those from TRUSTe and BBBOnline, seek to codify best practices into a form of self-regulation and I examine them here, along with an implementation of seal technology in email. I will also discuss an Internet "community" response to Web site privacy known as the Platform for Privacy Preferences Project, or P3P for short.

Free Assistance

I like to describe the Web as a self-documenting phenomenon. From its earliest days, one of the most popular uses of the Web has been to find out about the Web. This certainly holds true when it comes to privacy and Web sites. Judicious use of your favorite search engine will locate a host of references and resources, from "privacy advocates" to "privacy Web." Searches tend to be particularly productive in the area of privacy regulations, such as HIPAA, and privacy policy. I have provided what I think are the most useful Web privacy references in the Sources section at the end of the book. To make sure you are up to date you should subscribe to some of the privacy news lists that are available. Again, my favorites are listed in the Sources section.

Sources of free assistance with Web site privacy policy were discussed in Chapters 6. These include the Direct Marketing Association (DMA), the Organization for Economic Cooperation and Development (OECD), BBBOnline, TRUSTe. Free policy editors for P3P, a technology discussed later in this chapter, are available from IBM and Privacy Council. Of course, there is no shortage of Web site privacy policies that can be read freely for reference and inspiration (just remember not to put anything in your policy that is not accurate or appropriate).

One interesting privacy tool, the Tivoli Privacy Wizard, is available free from IBM's Web site. This program transforms written privacy policies into electronically expressed privacy rules that can be understood by enterprise privacy monitoring and enforcement software or exported to standards-based privacy rule sets, such as P3P. You can import existing privacy policies or use the tool's graphical user interface to create or refine privacy policies based on laws or organizational requirements. The tool provides a way to define who can use what data for what purpose and provides automatic links to enterprise privacy management software.

Commercial Privacy Products

While a privacy policy generator can get you started, the products in this section aim to go a step further and help you implement and enforce your privacy policies.

PrivacyRight

The company PrivacyRight offers its TrustFilter system to simplify the management of sensitive customer information. It can integrate with an enterprise's existing customer information management structures, and it helps to provide a single, secure point at which to access a consumer's collected information. The TrustFilter suite consists of a permissions engine and an audit server. The permissions engine is a Java-based enterprise middleware platform that enforces privacy regulations, policies, and preferences by evaluating requests for data and comparing them to dynamic-access-control rule sets. The permissions engine includes a suite of privacy rules tailored to comply with specific legislative requirements. Support for multiple rule sets facilitates compliance with conflicting privacy legislation (such as when state rules supersede federal rules).

The audit server is designed for IT administrators and consumers to help in managing the permissions and usage of consumer data. It records functions of the TrustFilter system, authentication details for disclosure requests, and whether requests were permitted or denied. An audit report can be delivered to authorized users through the Web or in hard copy, as required. Administrators can view reports detailing the status of policy change notifications and authorization requests, aiding in compliance initiatives.

IDcide

The PrivacyWall product family from IDcide is designed to help you make sure your Web sites do not violate users' privacy. PrivacyWall thoroughly analyzes even the most complex Web sites and reports about everything that is crucial for the person in charge of privacy to know. For example, a PrivacyWall system shows all the personal questions asked anywhere on the site, warns about Web constructs that cause leakage of sensitive personal information, discovers Web pages that accidentally publicize personal information, and detects Web sites that are operated without management's approval or knowledge.

There are two products in the PrivacyWall family. The PrivacyWall Site Analyzer can be used remotely to analyze Web sites, either by you or by a consultant who has licensed the product. With it you can quickly understand the site's handling of personal information and define appropriate privacy policy. The PrivacyWall Site Monitor addresses the needs of in-house privacy and security officers. It is easily installed as a passive part of the infrastructure and provides continuous oversight of privacy compliance.

Watchfire

One company that has specialized in Web site management tools from a risk perspective is Watchfire. The company provides comprehensive website management solutions that analyze content to identify key issues that affect website operational costs, online risk, and user experience. Privacy analysis is thus included along with a variety of other factors that are important to the overall Web management task.

The company's WebXM product can scan very large and complex web environments while analyzing a broad set of site-related content issues. The product's content testing, analysis, and reporting capabilities should help you better control enterprise Web sites. At the same time, the product's functionality can be integrated into your existing Web production architecture and workflows. Users of the product can output reports showing a wide range of perspectives on key website issues. These include not only privacy, but also content defects, accessibility of content, and website standards compliance. In addition to providing WebXM as a product, Watchfire also offers WebXM Managed Service, a hosted website analysis and reporting management service.

Zero Knowledge Systems

Starting out in 1997 as a company offering privacy protection to Web surfers with its Freedom WebSecure product, announced in 1998, Zero-Knowledge has more recently begun offering companies an Enterprise Privacy Manager (EPM). This is software that allows a company to define, implement and centrally manage corporate privacy practices. EPM works with existing information resources, including customer and employee databases, Web servers, enterprise applications and access control systems to match the company's stated policies with effective privacy practices.

In addition to the EPM software solution, Zero-Knowledge also offers EPM Services, technical consulting, training and development that ensure the application fits properly within each unique business environment. EPM Services establishes the priorities for a company's enterprise privacy plan, analyzes its information-handling practices, and supports the efficient training and implementation of EPM.

Privacy Council

If you don't want to invest in the licensing fee for a privacy tool, or if you are short on personnel to address Web site privacy, you can hire someone to do some of the work for you. For example, Privacy

Council provides a service called Privacy Scan, a detailed examination of your Web site that provides the following information:

- An inventory of cookies on your Web site—including specific locations and life spans—plus P3P implications at a variety of settings and values.

- A comparison of apparent cookie behavior relative to the stated privacy policy.

- An interpretation of cookie conduits, combinations of cookies and forms, and the security implications of cookies.

- Security implications and specific recommendations regarding privacy practices in general, P3P policies specifically, and compliance issues.

Following the scan, experts at Privacy Council analyze the data, relative to industry laws and practices and the company's stated privacy policy. These experts then create a report that explains the findings, makes specific recommendations, and offers guidance on the next steps. Similar services are available from large consulting firms such as PricewaterhouseCoopers and IBM Global Services, or specialists such as ePrivacy Group.

Platform for Privacy Preferences Project

One Web site privacy tool that merits its own section is the Platform for Privacy Preferences Project, or P3P. This is not so much a product as a technology developed by the Word Wide Web Consortium (W3C). The goal is defined as follows:

> To provide a standardized set of multiple-choice questions, covering all the major aspects of a Web site's privacy policies.

Taken together, they present a clear snapshot of how a site handles personal information about its users. P3P-enabled Web sites make this information available in a standard, machine-readable format.

When someone visits a P3P-enabled Web site, using a P3P-enabled browser, the browser compares the site's privacy snapshot to the consumer's own set of privacy preferences. In this manner,

P3P is said to enhance user control "by putting privacy policies where users can find them, in a form users can understand, and, most importantly, enables users to act on what they see."

Since W3C also describes P3P as "a simple, automated way for users to gain more control over the use of personal information on Web sites they visit," there is something of a dichotomy between the implied automated comparison of site to user privacy preferences and the emphasis on users doing it for themselves. Indeed, this has led to criticism from privacy advocates who claim that P3P will not work because users will not want to read all of the different privacy policies they encounter; thus they will turn on automatic negotiation with broad settings so as not to slow down their surfing, much like users currently do with cookie settings and security settings.

Privacy advocates also feel that P3P sidesteps the question of what online privacy standards should be, and that could even be construed as facilitating the coexistence of a wide range of approaches to handling personal data, some of which may be invasive. Furthermore, P3P lacks support for the fifth of the five fair information practice principles: Enforcement/Redress. A site can claim to follow certain standards in principle while violating them in practice and still pass P3P inspection.

Thus it remains to be seen whether P3P will become a useful tool for Web site privacy management. Nevertheless, if you decide not to provide a P3P policy on your Web site you might still want to make sure that applications on the site that use cookies, such as adverts, will still function correctly when accessed via a default installation of Internet Explorer 6 (explained in the next section). For information on a number of tools that help you do this, check out the sources section at www.privacyforbusiness.com.

P3P in Internet Explorer 6

To give you a better idea of what P3P means in practice, consider how it appears to users of Internet Explorer 6 (IE6), the latest release (as of this writing) of Microsoft's free Web browser. IE6 implements a portion of the P3P standard and is being heavily promoted as supporting new privacy features and improved cookie filtering—that is, support for P3P. Users can configure IE6 privacy options on the Privacy, Content, and Advanced tabs in the Internet Options dialog box, giving users more control over cookies and more information on a Web site's privacy policy. These settings determine how IE6 acts when it encounters P3P-encoded privacy statements on a Web site.

When browsing a Web site, IE6 checks whether the site provides P3P privacy information. If it does not, the user does not receive any warning, but IE6 will still block any cookies according to the user's privacy settings. If the site does provide P3P privacy information, IE6 compares the user's privacy preferences to the site's P3P policy and decides whether to allow the site to set cookies or restrict them. If any cookies are blocked because the user's privacy preferences don't match the site's policy, a warning message pops up the first time this occurs, explaining that a cookie has been blocked. The next time that a cookie is blocked, a status bar icon is displayed. Here is the warning message:

IE6 includes six preconfigured cookies settings, ranging from Accept All Cookies to Block All Cookies, with the default set to Medium. Custom privacy settings can also be imported, but it is expected that most users will use the default setting.

The Medium setting automatically restricts cookies that use personal identifiable information for secondary purposes or transfer such information to recipients beyond the site being visited. This setting does, however, allow sites to use cookies to collect data that may be needed for product delivery services. The actual settings that constitute the Medium setting are as follows:

- Blocks third-party cookies that do not have a compact privacy policy

- Blocks third-party cookies that use personally identifiable information without your implicit consent

- Restricts first-party cookies that use personally identifiable information without implicit consent

Whenever cookies are blocked after the initial privacy warning, an icon appears in the browser's status bar indicating that IE6 has taken a privacy protection action because of a cookie. The user can click the icon to view a Privacy Report, as shown in Figure 9-1, which lists the content of the Web page. The Privacy Report provides a link to the privacy summaries relating to the content of any item in the list, as shown in Figure 9-1. Users can also request a Privacy Report at any time via the View menu.

Because IE6 is likely to make users more aware of privacy issues—in particular the use of cookies—and because it makes it easier for users to block certain types of cookies, your company will probably want to make sure that its Web applications do not trigger unnecessary IE6 interference.

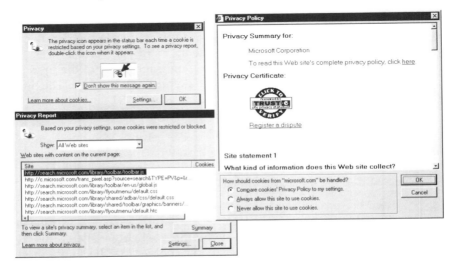

Figure 9-1 P3P dialog boxes in Internet Explorer 6.

Other P3P Software

P3P capability does not have to be built into a Web browser, it can simply be plugged into the browser, which it the approach taken by AT&T with its Privacy Bird software. This free software adds extensive P3P capabilities to a range of Web browsers, automatically searching for privacy policies at every Web site the user visits. Privacy Bird users can tell the software about their privacy concerns, and it will tell them whether each site's policies match their personal privacy preferences. The software displays a green bird icon at Web sites that match, and a red bird icon at sites that do not.

P3P in Practice

P3P aims to achieve "informed consent through user choice," whereby an individual can access sufficient information so that he or she can make an informed decision on whether to permit further use of personal data or decline further use of their data, helping to establish trust on the part of the user that personal data will be provided only to Web sites whose personal data use and disclosure practices are in accordance with the user's expectations. Moreover, that decision can be delegated to a software agent acting on behalf of the individual by design or default. The P3P protocol is intended to support negotiations in a wide variety of contexts, including the following:

- Implicit data provision (in particular the click stream, or series of pages visited at a Web site)

- Explicit data provision (such as answers provided by Web users in Web forms)

- Explicit data provision from an established Web user profile (such as a set of terms that reflect a person's interests and are commonly used in searching, and consumer-related information, such as contact and product preferences)

If your company decides to be P3P compliant, it needs to create a P3P version of the Web site privacy policy, which means rounding up a lot of information and definitions that are required by P3P. Someone will need to be tasked with categorizing all data captured and classifying all cookies used by the site. It is important to make a note of all data collected, what happens to it, who has access to it, and for how long it is kept. This information will be fed into a P3P generator that will create a machine readable version of the policy.

If the site is complex and uses third-party services, this could take several person-days and require an understanding of the business processes involved. On the plus side, this process creates a valuable document for future reference and site support. The information required by P3P includes the following:

- The organization that is collecting information

- The type of information that is being collected

- How the information will be used

- Whether the information will be shared with other organizations

- Whether users can access personal information and change how the organization can use it

- How disputes with the organization are resolved

- How the organization will retain the collected information

- Where the organization publicly maintains detailed information about its privacy policies

Fortunately, a P3P Policy Generator can be used to assist in creating a machine readable P3P-compliant policy file. A generator prompts for all the necessary information so that the policy is correctly and fully formatted in XML. Several of these generators are currently available (see www.privacyforbusiness.com for links to these). Based on the current P3P specification from the W3C P3P site, the following information is required by the policy generator:

- **Entity:** Who you are and how a user can contact you.

- **Disclosure:** Where your written, human-readable policy is located on your site.

- **Assurances:** What third party or law insures that you are doing what you say you are.

- **Data Collection and Purpose:** What data elements are you collecting and how are you using them. Any collected data has four defined classifications under P3P:

- **Data Category:** Fourteen data categories, plus "other," are predefined.

- **Specified Use:** One or more of six specified purposes can be assigned.

- **Recipients:** One or more of six possible recipient options can be assigned.

- **Retention:** Five options cover how long the information is being retained, ranging from no retention to indefinite retention.

After the necessary information has been entered into the P3P generator, the generated file is saved as policy1.xml. If multiple P3P policies exist, they are numbered policy2.xml, policy3.xml, and so on. The generator also creates a policy reference file, called p3p.xml, which contains any includes and excludes, as well as any more specific task classifications that Web browsers will use to navigate the P3P policies and apply the correct policy to each page. Pages and whole directories can be included and excluded as long as all pages and directories are ultimately accounted for.

The P3P policy file or files, and the policy reference file, are then uploaded to the server's root directory. The P3P site at www.w3.org/ P3P/validator.html can be used to validate the site's compliance with P3P and report any errors. Once compliant, you can register your site as a P3P-compliant site with W3C P3P Initiatives.

P3P Action Plan

You first need to decide whether your site is going to be P3P compliant. If so, you should determine whether the current privacy policy complies with the P3P Guiding Principles Document; if not, you need to bring it into compliance. (If the site does not yet have a privacy policy, you can develop one that is compliant from the outset.) Bear in mind that the decision to comply with P3P is not without its risks, as outlined in the next section. A privacy officer or similar person should to designated to organize the task of P3P data gathering and documentation. Be sure that this includes a review of the directory structure of the site to ensure easy management of P3P include/exclude instructions. Also, review the status of all third-party services with regard to P3P.

One optional aspect of P3P should probably be addressed before firing up the P3P Policy Generator—the ability to respond to disputes from users. P3P allows, but does not require, the designation of one or more resolution methods. This can be your existing customer service department, an independent organization such as a seal program like TRUSTe, or processes that might exist under an applicable law—for example, in the UK, that would be the Data Protection Act of 1998. Because there are solid business reasons for having a dispute-resolution process in place anyway, it makes sense to include it in your P3P compliance.

Privacy Statements and P3P

You get a different take on privacy policies and P3P if you listen to some privacy advocates. They object to the fact that no enforcement or redress is required in P3P. Indeed, it is entirely possible to craft your P3P policies so they look good even if you have no intention of standing by them (of course, if you take this approach you risk the ire of FTC and other possible legal actions).

At the same time, the implementation of P3P in IE6 is construed by some privacy advocates to be a "forced adoption" of a flawed privacy standard. Some commentators have said that the P3P filters "punish administrators who fail to publish properly coded P3P privacy policies by blocking or impeding their cookies" (from Benjamin Wright, founding author of *The Law of Electronic Commerce*, Aspen Law & Business, 1990–2000). According to Wright,

> "The P3P coding language raises, for any corporation, government agency or other institution that uses it, a lawsuit danger. A privacy policy written in it exposes the organization to liability, with little or no escape. A privacy policy, even one written in computer codes, can be legally enforceable like a contract. In lawsuits filed in 1999, plaintiffs forced US Bancorp to pay $7.5 million for misstatements in a privacy policy posted on its Web site."

Wright sees Web site administrators facing a dilemma: how to satisfy IE6's technical requirement for P3P codes, while sidestepping liability. As a remedy, he proposes a legal disclaimer, written as a new code in the P3P syntax. The new code is DSA, short for "disavow P3P and any liability it carries." Web administrators are free to use DSA in "compact" P3P privacy policies. Administrators are also free to reference or repeat the following statement:

> The DSA token in a compact P3P privacy policy means this: The P3P codes and so-called P3P privacy policies we publish have no meaning and carry no obligation or liability. They are fictitious. We disavow any significance to those codes and policies and reject all aspects of the P3P protocol. We employ P3P codes only as technical switches to enable our Web site to function properly. Some Web browsers require those codes to trigger the function of certain cookies. Our use of P3P is completely unrelated to any privacy

or data policies that we may be bound to. For more information, see www.disavowp3p.com.

Here you have one possible solution to liability issues arising from P3P, although you should run it by the legal department before implementing it. It remains to be seen whether P3P matures sufficiently to meet its designers' original objectives or is discarded as a failed attempt to automate something that is more effectively accomplished by companies adhering to high standards and people exercising good judgment.

Privacy Seals

You will have seen numerous references to Web privacy seals in other chapters. This section provides additional information about the various privacy seal programs currently available. Evidence for the importance of such seals can be seen in these findings from a Harris Interactive poll conducted in February of 2002: 84 percent of U.S. consumers think companies should be required to submit their privacy policies for independent verification; and more than 90 percent of respondents said they would do more business with a company that had its privacy policy independently verified.

How Privacy Seals Work

The basic idea of a Web privacy seal is simple enough: your company licenses the seal from an independent organization, normally for a fee. You bring your company Web site into compliance with the standards represented by the seal. You place the seal symbol on your Web pages. When a user clicks the seal, a message verifies that the site complies with the standards represented by the seal.

Of course, the actual implementation of this simple idea is not so simple. From your point of view as the licensee, the company that wants to display a trust seal on its Web site, there may be a lot of work involved to "bring your site into compliance with the standards represented by the seal." Hopefully, you can use some of the advice in earlier chapters to get this work accomplished, but the scale of the task should not be underestimated, particularly if your company is just getting to grips with privacy. Companies that already have privacy policies and Web privacy statements in place may find the task less onerous.

The licensing organization that issues the seal also has a number of tasks it must perform if the seal is to be effective. If your company is thinking of licensing a privacy seal you should consider how the licensor handles the following tasks.

Develops standards: A seal will only be widely supported if it certifies licensees to a reasonable standard, one that licensees can meet, but which still commands respect from the target audience because it embodies desirable principles and requires appropriate behavior. This task requires a tremendous amount of effort. Numerous constituencies must be consulted, consensus must be formed, standards must be both legally formulated, and accessibly articulated.

Educates the public: A seal that embodies good standards will not be effective in promoting those standards unless the target audience recognizes the seal and understands what it stands for. Resources have to be committed to getting the word out about the seal and what it stands for.

Certifies licensees: A seal will not work if getting it is either too easy or takes too long. An infrastructure for expeditiously certifying the licensees is required and it must be administered effectively.

Prevents abuse of the seal: A seal that is hijacked or diluted by imposters and abusers will quickly become worthless. For the public to respect the seal it must be protected. Policing the seal requires both human resources and effective use of technology.

Enforces compliance with the program: A seal that is just a rubber stamp will not retain the respect of the constituency it is designed to serve. Licensees who violate the seal's standard must be dealt with, which can require legal, business, and PR skills. Sanctions must be sufficient to satisfy the seal's constituency.

Resolves complaints: A seal that succeeds in all of the above will set standards and acquire stature, but it will also act as a lightning rod for complaints and frustrations. A fair and efficient dispute resolution process must be put in place.

The importance of these tasks can be summed up by saying that the credibility of the seal must be maintained in order for it to be effective, clearly no easy task. That is why there are only a few successful seal programs.

TRUSTe

A non-profit organization backed by sponsorship and fees from many of the largest Internet companies, TRUSTe has developed the most widely recognized privacy seal so far. Statistics about the TRUSTe seal not only reflect this recognition, but also serve to illustrate the level of interest that Web users have in trust seals. An independent research firm found that by mid-year 2000, some 69 percent of U.S. Internet users recognized the TRUSTe Privacy Seal.

Furthermore, TRUSTe ranked among the top-three most recognized symbols, along with Visa and MasterCard, among the entire sample base, which included Latin America. In the same study, TRUSTe was identified as the most trustworthy symbol online among U.S. Internet users, with 55 percent of respondents indicating that the presence of the TRUSTe Privacy Seal increased their trust in the website. This placed TRUSTe above Visa, MasterCard, and Verisign. The TRUSTe seal program comprises three main elements:

- **Program principles:** Address the privacy practices and procedures that will keep your Web site in step with fair information practices.

- **Oversight:** The measures that TRUSTe takes to ensure that licensed Web sites adhere to posted privacy policies.

- **Resolution:** The role TRUSTe plays in resolving privacy concerns or complaints raised by consumers or TRUSTe with respect to your site.

After you have completed a formal application to become a TRUSTe licensee, a TRUSTe representative will review your site for adherence to the program principles, privacy statement requirements, and trust mark usage. A representative will then periodically review your site to ensure compliance with posted privacy practices and program requirements, and to check for changes to your privacy statement.

To help ensure the credibility of its oversight role, TRUSTe regularly "seeds" Web sites, tracking unique identifiers in the site's database. TRUSTe will submit unique user information to the site and monitor the results to ensure that the site is practicing information collection and use practices that are consistent with its stated policies. Oversight is also supported by consumer reporting. TRUSTe provides a convenient online watchdog reporting form that anyone can use to report suspected violations of trust mark misuse. A key element of the success of the TRUSTe program is the ability of the community at large to report violations of posted privacy policies, misuse of the TRUSTe trust seal, or specific privacy concerns pertaining to a licensee.

Specialized Seals: Several privacy seal variations are available, including the Children's Privacy, E.U. Safe Harbor, and E-Health seals from TRUSTe. Other seals can be used to bolster your site's credibility, such as BBBOnLine's Reliability Seal that attests to an online merchant's customer service record. The Health On the Net Foundation (www.hon.ch) manages the HONcode seal for medical and health Web sites in support of a code of conduct for reliability and credibility of healthcare information on Web sites.

BBBOnLine

The BBBOnLine Privacy program is operated by the Better Business Bureau. BBBOnline awards a privacy seal to businesses that have been proven to meet the high standards set in the program requirements. These requirements include: posting of online privacy notice meeting rigorous privacy principles, completion of a comprehensive privacy assessment, monitoring and review by a trusted organization, and participation in the programs consumer dispute resolution system. For more information see www.bbbonline.com.

Email Privacy Technology

Privacy seals definitely help Web sites demonstrate their commitment to privacy standards. If your customers come to you mainly through your Web site, displaying a privacy seal will provide them with privacy reassurance. But what about contact through email?

Placing a privacy seal in email sounds like a good idea, but you can't just take a Web privacy seal and insert it into messages.

First of all, the organization that licenses the seal has to decide what exactly it stands for. Obviously it stands for "respect for privacy," but what does that mean in terms of email practices? Then there is the technical question of how the seal will be placed in the message—the design specification for a seal that sits on a Web page and looks good in most browsers is a lot shorter than for a seal that is placed into an html email message that will look good in all email clients. For a start, a greater variety of email clients are in widespread use today than Web browsers, not to mention the fact that many people still don't want html messages.

These problems pale in comparison with the challenge of preventing an email privacy seal from being abused. From the abuser's perspective, a Web site is a relatively static target. If I want to give my Web site at fakebiz.com a false air of respectability it is easy enough to place a copy of a legitimate privacy seal on the site. But as soon as anyone figures out I am not a licensed user of the seal, I am in trouble. I either have to remove the seal or move my Web site, which is not that easy if I rely on people finding my company at that address; not to mention the fact that the seal licensor already has an open and shut copyright and trademark infringement case against me.

Spammers don't have the same limitations, since most of their scams are already fleet of foot. Stopping them from using fake seals is a serious technical challenge. So far there has only been one serious response to this challenge, using a technology called Postiva, described in the next section.

Trusted Senders?

The non-profit organization that created the most widely recognized Web privacy seal, TRUSTe, also puts its name on a privacy seal for email through the Postiva Trusted Sender Program. Commercial emailers who participate in the program place a unique trust "stamp" at the top right of each email they send out, as shown in Figure 9-2.

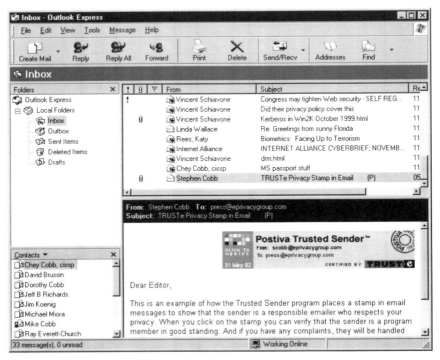

Figure 9-2 Postiva stamped email in Microsoft Outlook

The stamp signifies to the consumer on the receiving end that the message is from a trustworthy company that respects consumer privacy. The TRUSTe logo appears prominently in the stamp, along with the date that the message was stamped and the email address of both sender and intended recipient. This stamp is known as a *Postiva Trust Stamp* because it is created with ePrivacy Group's patent-pending Postiva technology, which uses encryption to defeat would-be impostors and enables the message recipient to perform an interactive verification of the message at a special Web site, www.postiva.com— all without any need for plug-ins, downloads, or modifications to standard email clients.

The Postiva Trusted Sender program was entering the field test phase in the summer of 2002 at some very large commercial mailers, including Microsoft's MSN. The software that performs the message stamping function is delivered to licensees on a plug-and-play appliance, which can be dropped into an existing email server configuration with relative ease and few modifications. The hardware is optimized to enable a large number of messages per second to be individually stamped and dispatched.

Each stamp is unique and the information encoded into it enables both the recipient and licensor of the seal program to verify that the seal is genuine. Anyone who receives a stamped message that cannot be verified at postiva.com is able—with just a few clicks—to report the violation. Since violators are breaking well-established trademark and copyright infringement laws for which there is strong international policing and support, there is no need to rely on new or untested anti-spam laws for prosecutions (fines for intentional violations of trademark laws are in the seven-figure range, and there is provision for some serious jail time as well).

Although no special software is required for recipients to verify stamped messages, or for ISPs and ESPs to deliver them, both ISPs and ESPs can benefit from installing the free Postiva Distributed Verification software. This allows the ISP or ESP to automatically verify the Postiva Trusted Sender messages it delivers to its customers, guaranteeing that they are authentic and from program licensees in good standing. The ISP or ESP can also flag such messages for recipients, as shown on the next page in Figure 9-3, where you can see messages flagged by Mailshell, a leading anti-spam ESP which was the first to install this system.

For consumers, Postiva Trusted Sender provides a convenient way of separating junk mail from legitimate commercial email. Postiva Trusted Sender also provides a guaranteed means of halting future mailings and gives easy access to a complaint process that is handled by an experienced and independent third-party, TRUSTe. For companies, Postiva Trusted Sender offers benefits in four areas:

Promotes Email Best Practices: There is broad industry and consumer consensus behind the Postiva Trusted Sender program, as evidenced by the range of organizations and individuals who have supported and endorsed it.

Provides an Email White List: Many ISPs are not comfortable with the current state of anti-spam filtering because of the incidence of "false positives," which have been described as "collateral damage

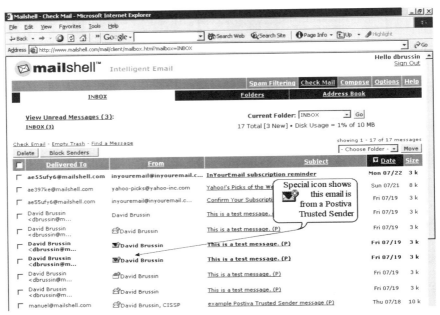

Figure 9-3: Mailshell identifies Postiva Trusted Sender email

in the war against spam." Just as it only takes one offended recipient to brand a company a spammer, it only takes one blocked message to brand an ISP many things, including an opponent of free speech. The Postiva Trusted Sender program creates a real-time, certified white list that ISPs can honor with little risk of criticism from either senders or recipients.

Bans Bogus Email: A company that adopts Postiva Trusted Sender for its customer email can, at a stroke, repudiate any brand-diluting email abuses of its good name. Government agencies and other self-certifying entities can even use the Postiva technology to create their own easily enforceable, spoof-proof seal of approval.

Provides an Open, Extendible Architecture: The technology behind Postiva is based on the principles of openness and extensibility. As the technology is deployed its capabilities can be expanded to deliver even more benefits to email, such as even greater privacy.

How quickly this technology will be adopted remains to be seen, but it has already proved that the private sector can deliver innovative and self-regulatory solutions to privacy and email problems.

CHAPTER TEN

SUMMING UP

0101011011100110111110100101110010101011011011

"Information is really the currency of the relationship with our customers, and trust is a key part of that relationship."

—Peter Cullen, CPO, Royal Bank of Canada

10: Summing Up

Congratulations! You have reached the final chapter. If you have read all of the other chapters on your way here you are now up to speed on the privacy issues that businesses face with respect to Web sites and email. For those who didn't read their way here, I should warn you that, while this chapter *is* a summing up, it is not a substitute for taking in the other chapters. As I warned in Chapter 1, these last few pages contain a certain amount of pontificating about what all of this means for businesses and why privacy can be good for business.

Great Exposure

Beginning in about 1996, a growing chorus of voices told companies that a presence on the World Wide Web would give them "great exposure." The phrase was used for years—by everyone from academic business gurus to Wall Street analysts—to describe this new ability to reach, at relatively bargain rates, a rapidly expanding worldwide audience. Apart from a handful of "paranoid" security experts, nobody seemed to get the double meaning. Then came the Web site defacements, the denial of service attacks, the hacker penetrations, the programming errors, and the avalanche of spam.

Today, there is a much better, and broader, understanding of the risks involved in "exposing" a company to the World Wide Web. But just as some companies "got" the security risks of a Web presence before others, and thus got a head start on doing something about them, so it is with privacy risks today. The companies that tackle this issue first are going to establish leadership positions that will be worth serious money.

When you want to talk serious money you should talk with a bank. An interesting bank to talk with is the Royal Bank of Canada, whose CPO, Peter Cullen, has been quite vocal about the value of privacy. The Royal Bank of Canada is a diversified financial institution that figures the shareholder value of its consumer and retail business to be about $9 billion (in US dollars). For several years now, the Royal Bank of Canada has taken a privacy positive stance, re-engineering its IT systems to track customer privacy preferences, insuring that they are respected by all bank departments, affiliates, and partners. Through surveys and other research, Royal Bank of Canada has determined that 7 percent of the demand for the bank's consumer and retail business is driven by privacy. That values privacy at $630 million!

Security and Privacy: If your company "gets" security, does that mean it also gets privacy? Not necessarily. Security focuses on "ensuring that information is conveyed where it is intended, as it is intended." That's a quote from a KPMG report on privacy published in 2001, titled *A New Covenant with Stakeholders*. The report notes that: "An information systems architecture enables information and transactions to stay private. An organization can have security without privacy, but privacy is impossible without security." I agree, although I usually put it like this: Security is about how you control information. Privacy is about who controls information.

Now that the days of easy dot-com money are behind us, a 7 percent increase in shareholder value should get people pretty excited; but if it doesn't, try thinking about a 17 percent loss. After all, you have to figure that failure to be privacy positive comes at a price. One company's 7 percent gain is another company's 7 percent loss, and that's just if the company losing out is privacy neutral. Failure to manage privacy effectively leads to damaging privacy incidents, and we have seen such incidents produce an immediate 10 percent drop in shareholder value.

The Blame Game

Back in 1999, Scott McNealy, the CEO of Sun Microsystems said, to a group of reporters, something like: "You already have zero privacy anyway, so get over it." Various versions of that quote—and Mr. McNealy's last name—rapidly populated articles and presentations about privacy, most of which made no mention of the original context. That context was frustration at announcing a new product, JINI, then having to field questions about the one thing it can't do— guarantee absolute privacy of personal data—rather than the many things it can do, such as make vital data instantly available across a wide range of hardware, software, and networks.

A lot of people in business can relate to Mr. McNealy's frustration with those who have turned privacy into an absolute. While the potential to abuse information technology such as Web sites and email is a genuine cause for concern, foolishly equating privacy with anonymity—somehow forgetting that you cannot participate in society unless you share information about yourself—does nobody any good. As I said in Chapter 1, the reason that privacy on the Web is such a big challenge is that nobody yet understands exactly what privacy means in the context of today's highly interconnected, heavily computerized, data-dependent world. About the best we can say is that privacy in the information age is a work in progress.

Light Down Under: When Scott McNealy addressed the National Press Club of Australia in September 2000 he explained what he meant by that zero privacy remark. Here is a verbatim transcript: "If you get hit by a truck, you want somebody to have your medical records. If you cannot tell them the combination to your safe or where your medical records are kept, you have a problem. In effect you want your medical records to be available online out over the Internet. You want every ambulance driver to be able to unlock it. So that is a little risk you take. Every ambulance driver might be able to tap into your medical records. Get over it. That is better than getting hit by a truck and dying."

Of course, if you are the sort of person who thinks corporate America is only out to steal people's wallets and ruin their lives, you are unlikely to be swayed by my assertion that most businesses actually want to respect the privacy of their customers, particularly if that is what their customers want. The problem is that we, as a society, simply haven't finished our homework on this one.

In other words, we are not yet at the point where a significant percentage of consumers have articulated specific Web and email privacy demands that businesses have chosen to reject. As Rob Leathern, a Jupiter Research privacy analyst recently observed, "Neither consumers nor businesses effectively address online privacy issues." He was reflecting on a Jupiter Media Metrix report that found more than 80 percent of U.S. consumers would give out personal information in exchange for small rewards, while at the same time nearly 70 percent said they were concerned about their privacy online. They might be concerned, but 60 percent admitted that they did not read privacy statements before handing over personal information to Web sites (not helped by the fact that a lot more than half of consumers surveyed found online privacy statements difficult to understand).

Survey Says: In exchange for as little as a $100 sweepstakes entry, some 82 percent of online consumers are willing to provide various forms of information to Web sites where they haven't yet made purchases. The percentage willing to offer email addresses, full names, household incomes, and phone numbers are 61%, 49%, 18%, and 19%, respectively. Over one third would provide a user name and password for a sweepstakes entry, even though more than half of online consumers—in a different study—said that they use the same user name and password wherever they go online (Jupiter Media Metrix report *Online Privacy: Managing Complexity to Realize Marketing Benefits*, June, 2002).

Yet I don't think that you can simply blame online consumers and their mixed signals about privacy for the current situation. Companies can, and should, do more to educate the public about online privacy.

After all, until a broader consensus exists about online privacy, no company can claim to have all the answers. The goal is to arrive at those answers, and have your customers with you when you get there. I also think it would be a big mistake for any business to use consumer confusion about privacy as an excuse for not acting. There is little doubt that, as several studies have concluded: without privacy and security enhancements, potential business will be lost.

According to a report in May, 2001, by Cyber Dialogue (now Fulcrum Analytics) some 82 percent of online consumers said a website's privacy policy is a critical factor in their decision to purchase. An even greater percentage had refused to provide information online at some point because they were unsure how it would be used by the company that asked for it. But the same study found the first privacy paradox to be very much alive— more than half the respondents said they were more likely to shop at a site that offers personalization.

The Privacy Paradox: The first privacy paradox, as stated in Chapter 1, is a reluctance to divulge personal information despite a desire for personalized products and services. That's why trust between consumers and companies is critical to solving the problems described in the book. For example, people like Privacilla's Jim Harper have pointed out that spam exists in large part because email marketers know little or nothing about the interests of potential customers: "it is difficult to reconcile spam—emails broadcast to unknown people nearly at random—with the heart of the privacy concept, which is too much personal information being available too widely." In other words, if people had a way to share more information about themselves without it being misused or abused, they could get more of the personalization they want, and less of the stuff they don't want. That kind of sharing requires trust. Right now, some companies are working on the technology to enable and enforce that trust.

Final Checklist

Throughout the preceding chapters I have endeavored to described the many ways in which privacy concerns can impact a company Web site. Armed with the tools, techniques and strategies that I have described, you should be ready to make privacy a strong point—for both your Web site and your business—rather than a potential source of embarrassment, bad publicity, or legal action. Remember, the two keys to delivering on the privacy promises your Web site makes are good security and full awareness on the part of all who handle personal information that it should indeed be handled with care.

I leave you with two final checklists to consider. The first is advice from Jupiter Media Metrix on how companies should address privacy issues:

- Adopt a segmentation approach to identify groups of consumers that are most likely to respond to privacy marketing—defined as messaging intended to allay consumer privacy and security fears and promote differentiation based on conservative data collection and use policies.

- Proactively communicate and promote privacy and security policies and capabilities.

- Emphasize transparency, security and accountability in both online and off-line consumer communications.

- Create a privacy council with representation across business units and increase awareness of privacy and data issues at both the senior executive and rank-and-file employee levels.

And here is a list for Web site managers that I put together with my brother, Mike:

- Document all the personal data collected by your Web site (include data that you log, such as IP addresses of visitors, information that you record for cookies, Web bugs, and so on).

- Find out who in your organization is responsible for privacy and establish a communication channel with them.

- Make sure a readily accessible privacy statement is posted on your Web site to tell visitors what private data you collect and why.

- Review the privacy principles and laws in Chapters 3 and 4 to determine whether any of them need to be addressed specifically by your Web site's privacy statement and/or information collection and handling procedures.

- Review the procedures in place on your Web site to protect any private data you collect, up to or beyond any of the applicable standards mandated in the relevant legislation.

- Offer visitors to your Web site a way to contact you regarding privacy concerns they may have about your site.

- If your Web site sells goods or services, consider joining a privacy seal program to provide visitors with third-party proof that you have appropriate privacy policies in place.

- If your Web site collects email addresses for further communication with visitors/clients, make sure appropriate policies are in place for using those addresses, such as documented opt-in permissions and accessible opt-out provisions.

- Conduct an internal privacy audit of your Web site to uncover anything you might have missed.

- Arrange for an external privacy audit of your Web site to uncover anything else you might have missed.

SOURCES

For updated web links visit www.privacyforbusiness.com
where you will find the following sources plus many more
that could not be included here due to space constraints.

SOURCES

Model Privacy Statements and Policy Generators

Better Business Bureau Online sample Privacy Notice
www.bbbonline.org/privacy/sample_privacy.asp

TRUSTe Model Privacy Statement
www.truste.org/webpublishers/pub_modelprivacystatement.html

Direct Marketing Association Privacy Policy Generator
www.the-dma.org/library/privacy/creating.shtml

OECD Privacy Policy Generator
cs3-hq.oecd.org/scripts/pwv3/pwpart1.htm

ESRB Privacy Statement Privacy Composer
www.esrb.org/wp_composer.asp

Privacy Principles

HEW Records, Computers and the Rights of Citizens Report
aspe.hhs.gov/datacncl/1973privacy/tocprefacemembers.htm

OECD Guidelines on the Protection of Privacy and Transborder
Flows of Personal Data
www1.oecd.org/scripts/publications/bookshop/
redirect.asp?pub=932002011P1

FTC Fair Information Practice Principles
www.ftc.gov/reports/privacy3/fairinfo.htm

US/EU Data Privacy Directive Safe Harbor
www.export.gov/safeharbor/

Privacy Laws

COPPA: Children's Online Privacy Protection Act
www.ftc.gov/ogc/coppa1.htm

COPPA Compliance (at FTC)
www.ftc.gov/bcp/conline/pubs/buspubs/coppa.htm

G-L-B: Gramm-Leach-Bliley or Financial Modernization Act (pdf)
http://eprivacygroup.com/sources/glbfma.pdf

FTC Page on G-L-B and Financial Privacy
www.ftc.gov/privacy/glbact/

G-L-B Privacy Rule (pdf)
www.ftc.gov/privacy/glbact/

HIPAA: Health Insurance Portability & Accountabilty Act
aspe.hhs.gov/admnsimp

FHCA HIPAA site
www.hcfa.gov/medicaid/hipaa/

Findlaw on HIPAA
hippo.findlaw.com/hipaa.html

The E.U. Data Protection Directive
www.cdt.org/privacy/eudirective/EU_Directive_.html

U.S./E.U. Safe Harbor at Commerce Department
www.export.gov/safeharbor/index.html

Additional privacy laws at PrvacyLaw.Net
www.privacylaw.net/priv_stat.htm

Privacy Tools

TRUSTe seal programs
www.truste.org/programs/index.html

BBBOnline Privacy Seal
www.bbbonline.org/privacy/

HONcode seal
www.hon.ch

P3P at W3C

www.w3.org/P3P

P3P tools
www.p3ptoolbox.org

Privacy and Online Organizations

Internet Alliance
www.internetalliance.org

Electronic Privacy Information Center
www.epic.org/privacy/privacy_resources_faq.html

Privacy Alliance
www.iab.net/waa/press/privacy_press.htm

Privacy Officers Association
www.privacyassociation.org

FTC on privacy
www.ftc.gov/privacy/index.html

COPPA information from coppa.org
www.coppa.org

Gramm Leach Blilely information
www.privacyheadquarters.com

CIO Magazine Privacy Center
www.cio.com/forums/security/

European Union and International

EU commissioned study of spam
www.cr-international.com/spamsummary.pdf

Comments on EU Data Protection Directive from American Chamber of Commerce in Belgium
www.eucommittee.be/pop/pop2001/Icts/icts42.htm

ASP group faults EU laws
www.aspnews.com/profiles/technologies/article/0,2350,4451_707811,0

Detailed implementation of UK Data Protection in Universities

www.jisc.ac.uk/pub00/dp_code.html

Agencies in the E.U. and Other Countries

Australia — Privacy Commissioner
www.privacy.gov.au

Austria — Datenschutzkommission - Austrian Data Protection Commission

www.bka.gv.at/datenschutz

Belgium President — Consultative Commission for Protection of Privacy

www.privacy.fgov.be

Canada — Privacy Commissioner for federal institutions
www.privcom.gc.ca

Denmark — Registertilsynet - Danish Data Protection Agency

www.registertilsynet.dk

Estonia — Estonian Data Protection Authority
www.dp.gov.ee

Finland — Data Protection Ombudsman for Finland

www.tietosuoja.fi

France — National Commission for Freedom of Information

www.cnil.fr

Germany — German Federal Privacy Commissioner
www.bfd.bund.de
Greece — Greek Data Protection Authority

www.dpa.gr

Hong Kong — Office of the Privacy Commissioner for Personal Data
www.pco.org.hk/

Isle of Man — Data Protection Registrar
www.gov.im/odpr/

Italy — Italian Data Protection Authority
www.dataprotection.org/garante

Lithuania— Lithuanian Data Protection Inspectorate

www.is.lt/dsinsp

Netherlands — Data protection/privacy commission for the Netherlands
www.registratiekamer.nl

New Zealand — Data protection/privacy commission for New Zealand
www.privacy.org.nz

Norway — Norwegian office for data protection
www.datatilsynet.no

Portugal — Data protection commission for Portugal
www.cnpd.pt

Spain — Data protection commission for Spain
www.ag-protecciondatos.es

Sweden — Data protection commission for Sweden
www.datainspektionen.se

Switzerland — Data protection/privacy commission for Switzerland
www.edsb.ch

United Kingdom — Data Protection Registrar
www.dataprotection.gov.uk

Infosec and Data Protection Links

CERT® Coordination Center at the Software Engineering Institute, a federally funded research and development center operated by Carnegie Mellon University
www.cert.org

Infosec News is a good source of up-to-date information security information, articles, product reviews
www.infosecnews.com

Computer Security News Daily is another good source for information security news
www.mountainwave.com

Computerworld — Security Coverage
www.computerworld.com/itresources/rchome/
0,4167,NAV63_KEY73,00.htm

Security Focus offers security news on web site and through alerts services, to stay on top of software patches, vulnerabilities and so on
www.securityfocus.com

Information Security Magazine — a good news source
www.infosecuritymag.com/

Virus and Hoax Information
www.datafellows.com/virus-info

Collection of Security White Papers
www.iss.net/support/documentation/whitepapers.php

RSA Laboratories Frequently Asked Questions About Today's Cryptography, Version 4.1
204.167.114.22/rsalabs/faq/index.html

Recommended Reading

CPO Reading List on Amazon.com, created by Ray Everett-Church, recommends 18 titles for those who need to know about privacy.
www.privacyforbusiness.com/sources

Data Protection Reading List on Amazon created by Stephen Cobb.
www.privacyforbusiness.com/sources

Internet Privacy for Dummies
www.internetprivacyfordummies.com

Database Nation
www.databasenation.com